On completion of her initial studies at the Australian National University, Robbie worked as a teacher, a biochemist, a political activist and a feminist activist in Australia and the United Kingdom culminating in her election as a member of the Australian Capital Territory (ACT) Legislative Assembly. Thirty years working in the non-government sector and the New South Wales (NSW), Australian Capital Territory (ACT) and Australian governments followed. In 2004 she joined Regional Assistance Mission to Solomon Islands (RAMSI) as an advisor to the Solomon Islands' Prime Minister and Head of the Cabinet Office, and in 2008, she worked as an advisor to the national police (PNTL) in Dili, Timor-Leste. Robbie now lives in Canberra with her husband and works in the public sector. She has two adult children and four grandchildren.

For my contributing friends, their families and mine.

Robbie Henderson

Our Mothers

Austin Macauley Publishers™
London * Cambridge * New York * Sharjah

A CIP catalogue record for this title is available from the British Library.

ISBN 9781528999434 (Paperback)
ISBN 9781528999441 (ePub e-book)

www.austinmacauley.com

First Published 2021
Austin Macauley Publishers Ltd®
1 Canada Square
Canary Wharf
London
E14 5AA
+44 (0)20 7038 8212
+44 (0)20 3515 0352

While this book is about our mothers, it would be remiss of me not to acknowledge the important contributions made by our fathers to the lives of us all. Their stories are for others to write. Our mothers were as much their 'rocks' as they were ours.

We were a fortunate and privileged group of young people growing up in a developing capital city with its emerging national institutions. It was a safe place where we could walk into an unguarded Prime Minister's Lodge and chat to the inhabitants or run into parliamentarians in their shorts at the Manuka shops. We relished the political environment and learnt from it.

Almost all of us were lucky to be able to study or work at the Australian National University (ANU) and we are all profoundly grateful for this opportunity. The university provided us with an extraordinary education and opened our minds to new ideas and the importance of evidence, fairness and equality. It gave all of us the foundations to move into our future careers.

I would also like to thank Derek Abbott for his patience and advice about editing the text. I am especially grateful to Denis, Vee and Lou for their fine copy editing' and Peter Nolan for his design.

Table of Contents

Foreword

These essays fill an important niche in the discussions of 'mothers, daughters and sons'. The freshness lies in the approach: 'What perceptions do we daughters and sons have of our mothers'? and in the central question; 'Were our mothers happy'?

The authors are post-World War II baby boomers, now in their early 70s. Having attended one of two private single-sex schools or the Australian National University in Canberra, often in the same class, they are known to one another but have independently considered their mothers' aspirations and roles, each condensing their reflections into a few pages. Lengthier analyses are, of course, expected in full biographies, Jill Ker Conway's excoriating picture of her mother in *The Road from Corrain* (1989) being one such. By contrast, the intention of these essays is not to present detailed, fully referenced biographies—a difficult task in at least one instance when the mother was not at all sure of her date of birth, that on her passport being almost a decade out. The authors do not aim to present an unvarnished tribute to mothers or to pursue specific feminist interpretations but rather to see what emerges from uninhibited reflections.

Sixteen mothers, their daughters, sons and families are discussed here. They are all white, middle class, married to husbands in professional jobs, many with connections to Britain and experiences of living overseas and sufficiently well-to-do to afford to send their daughters and sons (most had fewer than four children) to private schools. This limited sample is a strength because it concentrates attention on a common link at a key stage in the lives of these families: their residence in Canberra, Australia's national capital, when it was not yet 100 years old.

These are cautionary tales, warnings against accepting generalisations and stereotypes. Mothers, seated in neat rows at Speech Days at two Canberra schools, dressed in hats and gloves and exchanging nods and smiles, may have given the impression that they had similar outlooks and expectations. Yet, a gulf in attitude existed between the mother who said that being 'a kept woman' (her words) was 'a gift she was happy to accept' and that of another who stressed that being a wife and mother was not her primary role and that her career came first.

On the central question, 'Was my mother happy?' categorical affirmations exist but are rare. Daughters and sons delve into the psychology of their mothers' personal relationships: the effect of being branded 'a scarlet woman'; of a Protestant marrying a Catholic; of forced moves with their husbands' jobs and of carrying the full responsibility for the home while the husband worked all day and night.

These reflections add important substance to fleeting references found in articles and obituaries. Journalist John Farquharson, noting the death in 1994 of prominent public servant Sir Fred Wheeler, remarked: "His devotion to his work was legendary and that must have placed some restraint on his family life with his wife, Peggy, his son and two daughters. At the Public Service Board, meetings continued indefinitely, even until midnight." As readers of the essay on the Wheeler family will appreciate, a son's perception of the way his father's work impacted on his wife and family provides thought-provoking detail.

While sympathy might lie with the mother waiting at home, one contributor makes a valid point: "Men had such a burden of responsibility in those days being the only breadwinner that stress was the common result." Many felt that it reflected badly on them if their wife went out to paid work.

Today, counselling is offered for misfortune and stress of all kinds but the only recourse for many of these mothers and fathers was to adopt a stiff upper lip. No couple in this essay solved problems by divorce. Children comment that their mother's strong belief in 'duty' gave them the ability 'to rise to the occasion'. The authors do not pretend to know all the answers: "One never knew," they confess, "what she was really thinking."

A feminist critique might well conclude that they were silenced into submission, a valid conclusion in the case of one mother who, appealing to her own mother for help, was instructed: "You have made your bed; you just have to lie in it."

The authors raise challenging questions, especially in relation to how their own lives have developed: Were paid working daughters a threat to non-paid working mothers? How did mothers react when their daughters' political views differed from their own? When a mother valued a career over marriage and motherhood, how accepting was she of a daughter who chose the opposite role of wife and mother over the possibility of a degree and a career?

This book may provide a model for groups who are interested in investigating disparate personal or family experiences around a common theme. Consider also the possibility of the children of these authors embarking on a similar analysis of their parents! In this case, the approach designed by Robbie Henderson will deservedly have a very long life.

Dr Jill Waterhouse

Introduction

This book contains a collection of 16 stories written by a group of friends who met during school and university days. These short stories are about their mothers. While these women were from different backgrounds and some were born, or lived their early lives, in different countries, they shared some things in common. They were British by either birth or ancestry, they were middle class and they were young mothers during the latter part of World War 2, or shortly thereafter. They lived in Canberra during the 1950s, '60s and '70s, longer in some cases, and contributed to the social life of the growing city in a variety of ways.

The idea to collect these stories came when I attended the funeral of Jean Moran, one of the mothers featured in this collection. It is perhaps inappropriate to say one enjoyed a funeral, but this was the case with Jean's. It was a happy affair which captured the life of a good and interesting woman. As I listened to her eldest son, Michael, I thought how many other people, not present, would have enjoyed it too.

It also made me think of my own mother and the many mothers of friends who had been part of my growing up in Canberra. Many married during or just after World War 2 and their lives were inevitably shaped by that monumental event.

I was lucky enough to have remained in touch with a number of these friends who had been my contemporaries at the Canberra Church of England Girls Grammar School (CCEGGS) and the Canberra Grammar School (CGS), the then brother school, and later at the ANU. As most of us were now over 70 years of age, I thought that if these stories were to be written, the time was now or we too might be gathered up before they were passed on.

A number of the mothers were active participants in the war effort, either in Australia or in the UK and it was this aspect of their lives that was of most interest to me initially. As it happened, those who have contributed have put their own frame around the tales making it more a collection of stories about a group of women living through the early days of Canberra or its surrounds; Marion Walmsley in Yass; Eleanor Delaney in Crookwell and Jean Gulson in Goulburn.

During the war, these mothers either served in the forces, the nursing corps or joined the auxiliary services that were established in order to release men for combat roles. Jeanne Cooper and Mouse Saunders served in the Women's Auxiliary Air Forces (WAAF) in the United Kingdom and Africa and Marjorie Hinchliffe in the Signals Directorate on Garden Island in Sydney.

Quite a few went home to live with their parents and resume the role of dutiful daughter, and/or to volunteer for organisations such as the Women's Land Army to support agricultural production; my mother, Laurel Henderson, being one of these. Finding herself pregnant, Joy Hartnell also returned to the family farm in 1942 where she stayed for the remainder of the war.

Others worked in jobs which had formerly been filled by men. Marjorie Nichols answered the call for economics graduates to take the place of absent male public servants in Canberra where she worked as a Research Officer in the Bureau of Census and Statistics.

Despite the difficulties and hardships, they may have experienced at home, for many of these women, the war gave them a sense of purpose and unity; a time when people worked hard, pulled together and were liberated from rigid societal norms; a time when their contribution was valued. Regardless of whether the men returned or not, the women had experienced a measure of freedom and they were mostly going to be changed by it forever.

Most of the mothers were actively employed in the paid workforce before the war, Peg Wheeler as a clerk in T & G Insurance in Melbourne and Hilda Simpson as a teacher in Aberdeenshire in Scotland. Yet, despite their limited liberation, these women, with the possible exception of Hilda, still believed that marriage and the caring for children was their principal lot in life and that they would give up work once they were married in order to raise their children and take charge of the household. My father, amongst others, thought it was poor form if one's wife worked; even if she wished to do so.

Life in Canberra was a shock initially for many of these young mothers whose lives had been spent in cities, overseas postings or on farms. Being the women they were, they made the most of it, rarely complained and leant on others like themselves to provide the support systems that they had left behind when they came to live in a fledgling company town.

They always seemed to be busy. Their domestic lives were not boring. Gardening, music, sport and driving children around a town poorly served by public transport took up a lot of their time; for many organising social events and preparing food for lunches and dinner parties took up even more. Playing the piano was more than a just a hobby for some of these mothers. Ellice Fisher was a well-known accompanist and often heard on the ABC.

The 'physics mothers', Dot Nicholls, Dorothy De Salis and Nan Stewart were an example of those who drove a lot. They trekked along Mugga Way and back from the girl's school to the boy's school several times a week taking those of the girls who wanted to study physics to CGS as CCEGGS did not teach it. I for one have always been grateful to them.

I think I underestimated how difficult it might be for some of the proposed contributors to write about their mothers. The writing of the stories proved challenging for some as they raised forgotten or long buried and unknown events. Indeed, some of the women's deaths were too recent, too connected to others who would not have wished them to be told, or just too painful to tell. Those mothers will be remembered even if their stories do not appear here. There were also other stories I would have liked to obtain but had lost contact with those friends and their mothers over the years.

For some of us, writing about our mothers raised questions in our minds about how well we actually knew these women with whom we had spent a major part of our lives. Did we ever really talk to them about their feelings or did we just take them for granted? Did we ever recognise the value of their unpaid work for their families and communities?

As the stories rolled in and I read about the woman's diverse experiences, I was happy we had made this happen. I think the mothers would have been pleased to have been acknowledged. Some of the women's lives were exotic by any standard, others were more domestic; whatever they were, they were special to all of us. Without their support and instruction, we would not have been able to say 'my mother taught me that'.

I loved these tales, especially as the voices of their children come through in the telling. I hope you will enjoy them too. I was delighted that local Canberra historian, Dr Jill Waterhouse, who knows most of the children, and who attended CCEGGS with some of us, agreed to write a foreword.

Robbie Henderson

Chapter 1
Jean Mavis Moran (Née Frame)

Louise Moran

Lou and I met in Orientation Week at the ANU in 1964. She was 16 years old and I had just turned 17. She had been at boarding school in Sydney but quickly became part of a growing group of friends featured in this book. Despite being in different faculties, Lou and I clicked and managed to spend a lot of time together. Her house in Forrest was excellent for chats/coffee and parties providing we could escape her pesky younger brothers, Hugh and Michael, (both of whom turned into very nice men). Lou's mother, Jean, always had nice brownies and other delights for us. For many years, Lou's very sweet grandmother Mrs Frame lived there too. Many stories were passed on over coffee and cake. Lou and I spent a year together in Bruce Hall, sadly now demolished, and somehow managed to pass our exams despite all the distraction.

Robbie Henderson

"Ic, ic, pah boo," you say.

"Goo goo pah nunc," she responds. You are enthusiastic members of the Gugnuncs, followers of Pip (a small black dog), Squeak (a bossy penguin) and Wilfred (a white rabbit) who inhabited a newspaper cartoon in England in the 1920s and captivated my seven-year-old mother, Jean. Some 70 years later, she could still summon up her childhood delight in joining the Gugnuncs and learning their greeting signs—a G and an N tapped out in the then deaf sign language. We were looking at a portrait of Alfred Deakin in King's Hall, Old Parliament House in which he is curiously placing two fingers of one hand on the palm of the other. A Gugnunc pronounced my mother. A far better explanation than the more likely Masonic or other secret society description—and after all, Gugnuncs were a secret society too.

Little Jean in Reading

What's more, Jean said learning deaf sign language was actually useful (presumably why she taught me at the same age). She was playing with a friend in the latter's garden, a rectory in Reading, England, when an indigent man turned up, as often happened at rectories. The rector's wife asked him if he would like some food but after some false starts, it emerged that he was deaf and dumb. Jean stepped in, used her newly acquired deaf sign language which he fortunately understood, and one man got a good feed. It was probably the start of her long and prodigious career serving the community—and all because she was a Gugnunc.

Jean Mavis Frame was born in Reading, Berkshire, on 4 August 1918. She was an only child and, despite or because of that, a gregarious one. Hers was a happy childhood and she learned early the art and skill of friendship, interest in others and curiosity about the world, qualities that remained with her all the way to her death on 8 May 2018 aged nearly 98.

Jean's parents were Allan and Emily Louise (née Ford) Frame, comfortable, middle class people who were believers but not churchgoers. Her grandfather, William, had migrated south from Scotland in the 1860s in search of work, and founded the family business manufacturing men's clothing. He lived nearby and the two were close. His obituary noted: 'No Scotsman in distress ever appealed in vain to his generous heart'. After his death in 1928, people would come around to Jean's house, seeking the same support from her father. She inherited this practical ethic.

Jean in Reading—with her hands-on hips, as she did for the rest of her life

Two elderly ladies who lived next door to the Frames had turned their house into a small primary school, which Jean attended. She later (1933–1936) went to Malvern Girls College in Worcestershire which she adored and which had a major influence on her. She had fun. The girls played lacrosse and performed tableaux, the teachers encouraged learning and Jean encountered Anglicanism which became her spiritual home for life.

Jean was blessed with a remarkable memory and when, in 1991, we went to the school and were taken to her old boarding house, she could name every girl in her year and those above and below her in the photos shown to her. That same trip we went to Shaldon, a small, exquisite Georgian village in Devon where the family spent their summer holidays every year. As she talked, I could see her six-year-old self, happily bouncing her ball on the paving stones and between the walls of the narrow lanes while she headed to the newsagent (still there) to collect the morning paper for her father.

Malvern provided a good education but Jean was unsure what she wanted to do after school till a family friend described the role of a social worker and that was that. She trained as an almoner (hospital social worker) at Bedford College, University of London, commuting daily by train and, again, enjoying every bit of the experience even when she spent time in miserable digs doing placements at places like the hospital in Leeds. The course opened new horizons to her intellectually. In particular, she remembered the lectures of the noted philosopher Susan Stebbing, who lectured the social workers on 'punishment'.

Jean graduated just as the war started and there was a short period before she took up a permanent job at Addenbrooke's Hospital in Cambridge when she was briefly a member—an unsworn member—of the Army after Dunkirk, working for some weeks in the kitchen at a camp for the evacuated soldiers. Sometime in the late 1930s, she had a holiday with a Dutch family in Holland and met her first real love, an architecture student called Henk. In 1942, she received a letter from Henk's father saying he had been executed by the Nazis for being a member of the Dutch resistance. Jean almost never spoke about him but always kept his photo; it was only at the end of her life that she admitted how devastating Henk's death had been at the time.

Mostly, though, her stories of the war were all about her time at Addenbrooke's and the wildly eccentric folk who lived in her boarding house called the Hermitage, which was next door to Charles Darwin's lodgings. I regret we didn't get more of those stories on tape; they'd make a wonderful book. The stories of her work were more about the difficulties encountered by civilians facing illness and family disruption, and the wonders of the new drug penicillin whose remarkable efficacy she witnessed in her clients. Although the war must have shaped how her ideas about society developed, and it must have strengthened her conviction of the importance of community and helping others, the war as such never loomed large in Jean's conversation. Religion played a more important role one way or another.

Towards the end of the war, Jean met Patrick Moran at the Hermitage. That was quickly 'it' for both of them and they became engaged in months, marrying in September 1946. It was a tremendously happy marriage, a meeting of minds and interests and humour; we kids were very lucky.

Pat was a statistician who had graduated from Cambridge, spent the war in operations research and now headed into an academic career. He was also a Catholic and an Australian. Jean was an Anglican. In Michael's eulogy for my mother, he recalled:

> *I asked Mum and Dad if they encountered any prejudice, England being anti-Papist. Oh no, they said, for Mum to marry not only a Catholic but a Catholic from Australia was something so far beyond the range of normal expectations it was exotic. It was if she were marrying a Buddhist from Nepal.*
> *In those days, people who married Catholics were often expected to become Catholics. Mum used to say gleefully in her later years, "They never got me, they never got me."*

Nevertheless, she kept her promise to bring us up Catholic and...

> *She went to the Catholic Church loyally for the next 50 years. Dad used to say, patronisingly, that Mum was the best Catholic in the family. It never occurred to him that she might end up the only Catholic in the family.*

They settled in Oxford where Pat took up a post at the University. I was born in 1947 and Michael in 1950. As was the custom, and in some cases, a legal requirement, Jean gave up her job and life was full of babies, making friends, and coping with rationing. Back in Australia, the Australian National University was just getting under way and luminaries like Howard Florey and Mark

Oliphant went on recruiting trips to the UK and America to find bright young Australians and cajole them to come home and start a university. My father, then 35, accepted the post of foundation Professor of Statistics and we arrived in Canberra in 1952; the start of a huge adventure.

Canberra then had a population of some 25,000; housing was incredibly scarce, especially for anyone coming to a non-public service job. My parents had a choice of two houses for sale; they chose 17 Tennyson Crescent Forrest and it was the centre of the family universe for 64 years till we sold it, with much heartbreak, in 2016.

Being designed along the lines of a two-storey Worcestershire farmhouse, it was more familiar to an Englishwoman than the usual Australian single storey house.

It sat in half an acre of ploughed earth, with two enormous yellow box gums and a smattering of wattles. Challenge number one was creating a garden from scratch; at home, Jean had loved being in the garden but had never done any actual gardening. In Canberra, with my father deep into setting up his department, it was largely up to her. She was homesick, public transport barely existed, they had one car, and she had two small children. It would be too easy to say this was the making of Jean because the signs of her adventurousness, courage and willing to get stuck in were there from childhood. She got on with it, with gusto. A home was created, a garden laid out, and above all, lifelong friendships were started. Everyone at the ANU was in the same boat and that must have helped.

My younger brother, Hugh, was born in 1953 and within a couple of years Jean started on the two paths that dominated the rest of her life, apart from her family—social work, and the ANU. We never discussed whether she regretted having to stop working after she married. I think the adventure of marriage, new circles of friends and the recovery from wartime constraints probably overtook any such regret.

However, with the three of us safely off at school, Jean became increasingly active in the ANU and her profession of social work. Although there were times later on when she worked almost full time for the Council of Social Service, it was always as a volunteer. She never took a paid job, feeling she was financially comfortable and the Council was forever lacking in resources so it was an in-kind contribution. It also gave her an enviable independence in her views and approaches.

When University House opened in 1954, Pat became the first Bursar, so Jean became equally involved. The House almost immediately became the focus of social life for the academic staff of the four Research Schools. A room was set aside for the ladies, almost entirely the wives of Members, and in 1956, they established themselves formally as the Ladies Drawing Room. Four years later, the ANU Club for Women was set up with an overlapping but broader membership. Jean was a founding member of both; it was a new adventure and she loved it.

Many of the women, like her, had had a professional life before marriage, and they sought intellectual stimulation and challenge as well as social life in a new city. Through these two groups, they met incoming new staff and visitors and ushered them to new homes (or put them up when the homes were not ready); they swapped baby clothes, prams and household goods (Canberra's shopping facilities were few); they created social and intellectual events of great variety; and above all, they created the social setting, cultures and friendships that would make the ANU a real, vibrant, humming society.

Jean became a mainstay of the Ladies Drawing Room for almost 60 years. It was run by an elected committee; in practice, she did most of the administration for two decades, and was the ideal person to write its history in 2002. I had the managerial career in the family but I've long thought my mother would have run administrative rings round me had she joined the paid workforce. Quirky, not always logical, but she was extremely well organised, kept meticulous records, and was very good indeed at getting others to do what she wanted; always with a smile.

This ability played well into the roles she would take up in social work too.

In about 1954, Jean joined the local social workers' group, comprising a tiny number of qualified social workers, either from government ranks or people like Jean who were volunteers. Jean took on the task of compiling, editing and producing a directory of social service agencies on which everyone could rely for information about who did what and might help. She ultimately did six editions of a dramatically expanding directory. On occasions, paper was spread over the entire floor of our study.

There were very few qualified social workers in Canberra in the early 1950s and most practical work was done by church groups and other charitable bodies. In 1954, Jean joined a group who were trying to do something about the plight of families of ACT prisoners who were all sent to NSW prisons, often far away, and that of ex-prisoners who had returned home after completing their sentence. Originally called the Criminal Rehabilitation Committee, they helped families in myriad practical ways to cope without their imprisoned relative. I recall numerous Christmas Eves spent, decades later, driving all over Canberra to deliver Christmas hampers. Eventually, as Prisoners' Aid, the organisation's finances have been regularised as part of the justice system and a support worker is based at the courts. Jean was a member of the committee for 39 years, often its secretary, and continued to have a caseload into her 80s; it was a significant component in her award in 1993 of the Order of Australia Medal for 'service to the community'.

In 1963, Jean was a founding member of the Canberra Council of Social Service (now ACTCOSS). The small voluntary sector had been swamped by the population influx of the 1950s which continued to accelerate in the 1960s as government departments were moved up to Canberra. The need was overwhelming for overall coordination of services, and a strong voice to government to obtain adequate funding for them.

Jean and the redoubtable Ethel McGuire took on most of the administrative tasks in the first few years. The COSS had very little income so sales of the directory of social agencies which Jean produced were important to its continued existence. She volunteered behind the scenes at ACTCOSS for several decades, taking on a variety of administrative tasks and becoming a fount of knowledge on social services and networks of people, past and present. Her networks were amazing but she was never a public figure; it was always about practical help in private.

In 2013, 50 years from its creation, Jean was made the first (and still only) Life Member of the ACT Council of Social Service. Having refused always to speak in public (an excoriating experience in primary school), she summoned up the courage to give her one and only speech—and spent most of it extolling the contribution of Ethel McGuire rather than reflecting on her own work. Typical!

The church continued to play a part in Jean's life. She and Pat were members of a Catholic theology discussion group of St Christopher's parishioners which was formed after the Second Vatican Council brought fresh air into the Church. It became known simply as 'the Group' in Canberra and the friendship bonds that were formed were as strong as the debates were powerful.

When Vietnamese boat refugees began to arrive in Canberra in the later 1970s, the local churches got involved in helping them to settle, find jobs and so on. Jean and Pat sponsored two families and helped them with housing, furniture, schools and finding their way through the bureaucracy. Jean stayed in touch ever after; one of the now-adult children came to introduce his new bride to her; Christmas cards and gifts were exchanged, and one daughter visited Jean when she was dying.

Jean's life was comfortable but there were, of course, great sorrows too—especially when Pat died in September 1988—and difficulties of various kinds. She chose not to show her deepest emotions openly, or not very often; mostly it was laughter and a bubbling enthusiasm for life and people. These were the qualities which people referred to overwhelmingly at her funeral and in the many condolence letters we received from all over the country and around the world. The joy she found in life was contagious and her energy was prodigious.

It was a mark of the love and esteem in which my mother was held by her friends and colleagues, and indeed by me and my brothers' friends, that some 150 people came to her funeral.

Grandma Jean at Tulip Tops

Note: I'd like to acknowledge the wonderful eulogy delivered by my brother Michael at Mother's funeral in May 2016. I've borrowed (i.e. plagiarised) quite a bit from it.

Chapter 2

Doris (Dot) Nicholls (Née Price)

Helen McBride

Helen and I met in the middle of our high school years at CCEGGS. She arrived in Canberra from Karachi, Pakistan where she and her family had spent two amazing years. As one of the bike riders along Mugga Way, we became friends immediately. She was an interesting and easy-going person and a very good tennis player. I spent many pleasant times with her and her family at home in Red Hill. Her parents were generous people and fun to be around. Mrs Nicholls was always busy in the kitchen or driving one of her three daughters around the town to various activities including, inevitably, physics lessons. Helen's father taught us how to clean our shoes the army way!

When Helen and Denis Saunders became close friends, our social activities included those regular trips up and down Quiros St. At the end of school, Helen departed for college in South Australia. I missed her wise counsel and kind heart.

Robbie Henderson

My mother grew up on a farm out of Kadina in South Australia. I believed she was the eldest of five children, including twins, one of whom was handicapped.

She went to the local primary school until year 7, initially travelling by pony. Then, as her brothers and sisters started school, they travelled by pony and cart.

There was no secondary education available for my mother to attend, so after leaving school, she helped her mother on the farm, with the milking and other household chores.

In 1939, the local teacher at Kadina introduced my mother to Norman Nicholls from Wallaroo. He left a few weeks later for Duntroon, Royal Military College in Canberra. Nevertheless, they corresponded regularly and he returned to Wallaroo and visited her for a few days before becoming part of the first contingent to the Middle East at the start of WW2. He was to become my father.

They corresponded for 2 1/2 years; got engaged and Dad sent material for a wedding dress, telling Mum to be ready for when he arrived home. Mum received a telegram saying 'See you soon'.

No further information until he arrived on 19 July 1942. They were married on 22 July 1942! After a short honeymoon at Glenelg in Adelaide, Dad was posted to Rokeby, Puckapunyal near Seymour, in Victoria for further training.

Dot in her 'Going away outfit' July 1942

In order to see Dad, Mum had to border hop, via Mt Gambier by bus, next day to Hamilton, then train to Melbourne. Quite a journey for a woman who hadn't been any further than Adelaide in her life! She stayed with friends in Melbourne so she could see Dad every month when he had a weekend off. Whilst in Melbourne, she worked voluntarily with Red Cross.

Dad was posted to Canberra in 1942 or early 1943, so Mum border hopped again. Train to Wagga, then a big car to Canberra. She recalled going mushrooming in paddocks, now part of the ANU, and sitting on the bar of Dads' push bike. Another vivid memory was the cold winter! They put newspaper under their mattress to try and stop the draught.

Dot and Norm shortly before he died in 1999

In 1944, Dad was posted to New Guinea and I think Mum stayed in Canberra. Then in 1945, Dad came home for a few months before being posted to Camberley Staff College in England. Mum wasn't allowed to go with him as it was only a six-month posting. So she returned to her parent's farm at Kadina. It was during this time she discovered she was pregnant with me.

Dad's posting was extended by six months and then another six months making his posting 18 months in total! I was 10 months old when Dad first saw me. Together again in 1947, they then went to Melbourne but it was not for long. Dad was sent to Japan for several months; so more time apart. My two sisters were born in Melbourne.

Dot with her four great grandchildren, Jack, Annabel, Phillip and Seb (on her knee) February 2007

In 1953, Dad formed part of the Australian Military Contingent to the coronation of Queen Elizabeth II and as a result, was off to England again. This was another six months separation.

Dad's next posting was Enogerra in Brisbane with the 1st Battalion which was then sent to Korean War, supposedly for two years. Fortunately, peace was proclaimed and Dad was home in 10 months!

My mother was a supportive Army wife. Fortunately, my parents had a number of interesting and enjoyable postings together after lengthy times apart. This included two years in Karachi, Pakistan in 1959 as Armed Services Adviser, then back to Canberra in 1961 before taking up the role of Military Attaché in Washington DC for two years in 1965.

Mum loved the social life which was part of these postings. After Dad retired from the Army, they went to Port Moresby to live for four years, where Dad was engaged as the Police Commissioner. Mum had a lot of interaction with the local policemen's wives which she really enjoyed.

They had been married for 57 years when my father died in 1999. They had retired to Victor Harbor, where Dad fished and gardened and Mum played bridge and mah-jong. They were both happy.

Mum died in 2007, very content with her life, although in the early years when Dad was away so much, she probably wondered how the future would pan out. Dad was forever grateful for her support and, for a country girl with very little life experience, she coped very well.

In 1996, my mother called me aside and told me her father wasn't the man I had always assumed was my grandfather! My grandmother, who had died the year before, had had her out of wedlock, but bravely would not give her up. Several people wanted to adopt Mum, but my pint-sized grandmother wouldn't part with her!

I wish I had known this before my grandmother died aged 97 in 1996. What a brave woman in that conservative time. Very few people knew, or spoke of Mum's background, very unusual in a small country town. Even her half siblings didn't know until 1986, when an elderly aunt died and left all her nieces and nephews some money. As Mum wasn't her niece, she declined the money!

It came as quite a shock, as there were aunts, uncles and cousins I didn't, and still don't, know.

Helen and Flip with their children Georgie, Nick and Kate

Chapter 3

Dorothy De Salis (Née Pratt)

Anne De Salis

Anne and I met when we were nine years old when I started my schooling at CCEGGS. I think she was deputised to look after me. I remember she showed me all the grubs in the trees on my first day. It was a small school then and I was glad to follow Anne around. She was clever, good at sport and fun. I think those early school days together were important for developing our values and beliefs. Over the years, I learnt a lot from her and our paths tracked closely through university, the women's movement, Labor Party politics and the caring for small children. They diverged when, after being the first female in the senior executive in the Treasury, she became a high-flyer in the corporate world. Many excellent parties were held at her parents' house in Deakin when we were in high school. Mrs De Salis joined in the dancing. She always looked smart, was fun and, as we physics students discovered, a willing driver.

Robbie Henderson

My mother, Dorothy Pratt, was born in Mosman, Sydney on 28 April 1920. Her father, Fredrick William Pratt, was a journalist with the Fairfax Press & Sydney Morning Herald newspaper and later became the manager of the classified ads (Fairfax's 'rivers of gold'). He was a well-established, 42-year-old when she was born to his second wife, Gladys Maud Cates.

My grandmother, Gladys, was a pretty young dressmaker still living with her family next door to the Pratts. She was 14 years his junior and they were married two years after Claire, my grandfather's first wife, had died. This union created quite a stir dividing friends and family.

My grandfather already had a young son called Harold and my grandmother had to deal with his understandable resentment as she began her own family. Dorothy grew up with her older step-brother and her younger sister Margaret in their large, dark three-story house in St Elmo Street in Mosman. As kids, we tiptoed around our grandfather as he tended his prize-winning roses in their disciplined rows while Gladys spent time with an exotic orchid collection in the greenhouse.

Dorothy and Margaret were brought up to be proper young ladies but still managed to have fun. She was especially close to her mischievous cousin Patricia Morris, who was the same age. When she was 12 years old, Pat became a victim of polio and had to spend the rest of her life in a wheelchair. My mother was devastated. They remained firm friends and saw each other often despite living in different cities.

My mother was educated at Wenona Girls School in North Sydney where she was a boarder for several years. In 1936 in her third year, she became the school librarian and received a school prize the following year. She apparently worked as a librarian after leaving Wenona, although I was unable to find out where.

At the outbreak of WWII, Dorothy was still a teenager living at home, enjoying life playing tennis and attending parties with various beaus, under the strict eye of her father. Years later when I was helping her to sort her old photos, she held up softly faded pictures of her and several young men one after another saying in turn 'that one was killed in France' or 'he died over Italy' or 'he was captured by the Japanese'. Clearly, her cohort of friends suffered huge losses during the war, something that the survivors must have struggled with for the rest of their days.

Eric De Salis was completing medical studies at St Paul's College at Sydney University when he met my mother. Being a true romantic, she bemoaned the fact that Eric proposed to her when she was suffering from a heavy cold and 'looking dreadful' but the ploy worked.

They married on 21 June 1943 at St Clements Church in Mosman, with many jokes (repeated over the years) about it being the longest night. Because of war rationing, her mother made Dorothy's wedding gown from some beautiful cream satin brocade curtains, and she was attended by her sister Margaret and a flower girl dressed in similarly created confections.

Dorothy as a young woman

From 1944 to 1946, my mother lived at home while Eric served Australia in the AIF as a medical officer with the field ambulance service in Papua New Guinea and Borneo. He witnessed the horror of war and its aftermath as he desperately tried to patch up the wounded and dying. This affected him deeply, according to my mother, but he flatly refused to speak about his experience.

The only story we ever heard about his war, told many years later to his 10-year-old granddaughter, Nina, was one of hope. As one of the first Australian doctors to use penicillin in the field in Papua New Guinea, he described its effect as 'miraculous' in helping desperately ill soldiers to recover in a remarkably short time.

But there must have been some home leave as their first son, David, was born in May 1944 and two years later, I was born in October 1946 in Sydney. By then, Eric had resigned from the Army to join the Commonwealth Department of Health. His first job was in Townsville, much to my mother's surprise. Dorothy took their two young children to join him for several years but never really settled.

She returned to Sydney to have their third child Michael in October 1950. By then, Eric had been appointed Director of the Health Laboratory in Canberra and the family moved there to live in early 1951.

Eric's family had farmed in NSW for generations. His parents still worked the Weston Creek Valley where my grandfather grazed sheep and cattle, whilst my grandmother ran the household, cared for the poddy lambs and grew enough fruit and vegetables to supply the families of all three of her sons and some neighbours.

Dorothy (called Dort by her friends) and Eric settled into a small house in Turner and soon had their own flourishing vegetable garden. My father threw himself into his work, expanding the clinical diagnostic services and in 1952, introduced a Pap-smear screening service (one of the first in Australia). Although Mum had been trained in domestic science and arts, the constant demands of Dad's extended family, endless fruit and vegetable bottling and caring for her boisterous young children largely on her own wore her down.

Dorothy and daughter Anne 1954

Things did not go well when Dorothy suffered what was then called 'a nervous breakdown', which landed her in the infamous Kenmore Psychiatric Hospital in Goulburn off and on for over 12 months. A young lab technician, who knew the family well, was hired to look after baby Michael and help dad with us older children.

On her return home, Dorothy had to re-establish her relationship not only with her husband but also her children, one of whom hardly knew her at all. She did so with grace and aplomb but holding her own in the formidable De Salis clan, with their heraldry, titles and centuries long history, was never easy.

Soon they were planning to build their dream home in one of Canberra's then outer suburbs, Deakin. The architect designed, ultra-modern, flat roofed house faced north with huge glass windows to capture the sun. There was plenty of room for entertaining, including a specially structured dance floor in the second living room. Dort loved people and parties, music and entertaining so this home was perfect. After getting a mortgage to cover the £12,000 cost of the new house, the family moved there in 1956 and Dorothy and Eric set about raising their family and creating a show quality garden. Gardening had become a lifelong passion for them both.

In 1958, she and Eric spent a year abroad so that Dad could continue his studies and attend a world meeting of the De Salis clan in Switzerland. They boarded their two eldest children at the Canberra Grammar schools and Michael in the care of his aunt and uncle at Weston and missed them all madly.

Dorothy was a wonderful full-time mother and supporter of her husband and his work, although she longed for him to go into private practice. She spread sunshine and laughter wherever she could, supporting friends as well as a number of charities. Like many other mums, she worked for meals-on-wheels for years as well as at her children's schools. The traditional family Sunday lamb roast in winter and barbequed lamb chops in summer were constant highlights, as were the tennis and pool parties at the family property Weston.

Our close-knit family suffered a devastating blow in 1963 when my brother David was killed driving up to the mountains to join the family ski holiday. She wrote in her diary, 'Lost our eldest son, David, aged 19 in car accident. We all felt our lives were over too'.

As was expected at the time, the bereaved had to show a stiff upper lip and bear loss without open demonstrations of grief. Dorothy did this better than most but not without taking a huge toll on her own health. In order to assist the family's recovery, Eric arranged to take a temporary position at Australia House in London and the four of us set sail for the UK on Christmas Day 1963.

Dorothy struggled through the next 12 months despite lots of travel distractions (all painstakingly recorded in her travel diary) but returned home better able to cope. She resumed her busy life but clung to Eric and her children, even if she found us wanting in many ways. Increasingly, her criticism fell on my father, who retreated into his work where in 1968 he and another specialist performed one of the first bone marrow transplants in Australia.

After originally arguing that I was far too young to marry, she and Dad were delighted that I would complete my university studies and become Peter Field's wife. But she was horrified when Peter was posted to Washington DC in the United States soon after we were married in 1967.

My mother came to visit us but it was not until 1970 all was forgiven when her first grandchild was born and named David after his late uncle. Two years later, we returned home to live in Canberra and our daughter, Nina, was born in the Canberra Hospital. We continued to live near my parents, as did my brother, Mike, enjoying their support, holidays at Mossy Point, regular family gatherings and their stories as they were retold to their grandchildren.

Dort loved the new and was willing to give most things a try when she was young, although she came from a very conservative background. She liked Gough Whitlam and his It's Time campaign until it all went pear shaped 1974. She was a bemused supporter of women's rights although could never make sense of the poster 'A woman needs a man like a fish needs a bicycle'. She insisted on defending her daughter for working for that 'dreadful Mr Keating' (the then Prime Minister) despite my protestations that it was unnecessary.

After Eric retired, they decided that their beloved Deakin home was too big if they wanted to get out and about. They moved first to Waramanga, a suburb in the Weston Creek Valley, in 1983 and then to live out their days in Garran close to Red Hill in Canberra. Over the next decade or so, they created yet more glorious and productive gardens, travelled extensively, played a lot of bridge with friends and attended the University of the Third Age. By then, their children and grandchildren had moved away and visits became a regular feature of their lives.

Mum gradually became more and more dependent on Eric as her mind slipped away. My father was diagnosed with motor neurone disease but struggled on as his beloved wife's primary carer. After his death in 2002, she refused to come and live with me or Mike in Sydney and a network of professional and family supporters enabled her to live out her days in her home, as she wanted.

She died alone of a massive stroke on 27 October 2004 aged 84 years old. I think she may have blamed the war for many of life's disappointments but she still treasured her family and friends and was treasured in return.

Chapter 4

Ellice Fisher (Née Summers)

Bill Fisher

By the time we were all in our 3rd year of high school, we started to make friends with members of the opposite sex in our brother school CGS. One of the boys was Bill Fisher who lived in Deakin and rode his bike along Mugga Way to school each day passing a few of us (girls) who were riding in the opposite direction. Inevitably, we had to stop and chat. Parties at the Fisher's house followed shortly after, swimming in their pool, throwing mulberries and listening to music. Often the sound of the piano and someone singing scales could be heard floating through the air as Mrs Fisher taught her students. The Fishers were one of the first families to have a television. We would all troop around to watch TV in the dark, which is what people thought you should do then. Mrs Fisher and Dr Fisher fed and watered us. Mrs Fisher was a small and very funny woman. Dr Fisher and Bill took great delight in lifting her up and putting her on the kitchen bench from where she could shout but not descend. Bill was in our physics class. He was smart and a fabulous swimmer. He always knew what he wanted to do in life and he did it; a successful diplomat and Australian ambassador in a number of countries.

Robbie Henderson

Ellice was born in 1909, but lied about her age so often that she actually forgot it. In later life, she had Australian passports with Date of Birth in three different years, finally twelve years apart. On husband Norm's 80th birthday he, for some obscure reason or other, was digging around in past papers and found her Birth Certificate, and discovered there for the first time that her real birthdate was 1909, not 1914, as he had thought, let alone 1918, as her latest passport baldly asserted.

She was born in Toowoomba, to a single mother, father having departed 'droving', to a childhood best described as genteel poverty. But appearances were everything, and the extended family was quite well off in rural Queensland, which led to an elegant and rather formal social life of the 'tennis and dinner on the property' sort. She went to Glennie, one of Queensland's better schools, a tribute to her mother's mighty striving to give her a formal education. The formal part was more important than the education bit, her mother's firm view being that a properly brought up girl did not bother with sums and things—Music and French were enough.

It was indeed the music which dominated her future life; the piano, specifically. She later said she regretted that so much of her childhood had been locked away with the piano, endless hours of practising. In many respects though, it paid off. She became quite well known around the Darling Downs as a performance pianist. More importantly—much more importantly—the piano was a highly efficient way to social success. In those days of no other form of entertainment, especially in rural Queensland, standard after-dinner practice was for all to gather around the piano and sing. And at that piano: Ellice Summers, centre of attention, brightest of personalities, musical suprema. This was a role she loved and it came back for her, even more strongly, in colonial New Guinea and again in early Canberra. Perhaps only the arrival of TV in the 1960s killed off this highway to social success in places where there was not that much else to do.

Ellice married at a very early age. This was more or less a practical arrangement, her mother being 'very ill' and feeling that Ellice needed looking after in case left alone in the world. In fact, her mother lasted for another 20 years or so, and who knows how serious that illness really was. In any case, Ellice learned the lesson of strategic illness, and played that card herself whenever the occasion suggested.

That marriage did not last long, but produced one child, Lorelee in 1932.

Here, Ellice's life took a remarkable turn, geographically, personally, emotionally, stressfully. She re-found, so to speak, an old flame from Toowoomba days, Norman Fisher, a geologist of some renown. He was working in New Guinea Mandated Territory, first in Wau on the goldfields and then in Rabaul as the Chief Geologist and Volcanologist (work which saw him awarded a rare DSc). He used to say later that he had always had his eye on Ellice, but who knows how or when they met up again.

At least he was not married—but of course, she was, and that led to that most catastrophic of social deaths in rural Queensland: divorce. Not only divorce but, as was the case in those days, a divorce which required the offending couple to be 'caught' by the aggrieved husband. There followed therefore a highly structured drama, in which the aggrieved husband seems to have played a willing, indeed sportive, part. Ellice and Norm, attired in dressing gowns, ahem, sat in a room in a hotel where at the appointed hour said husband plus lawyer and photographer burst in upon them, ahah, to provide the necessary evidence required by a judge to get a divorce.

Well though the divorce went, not so well the social consequences. Norm's family disowned him. Indeed so fiercely did his mother take it that she never spoke to him again, never had any dealings with Ellice and never met the resulting family. In other words, life around the Darling Downs was far too unpleasant to contemplate staying, both for Norm in the face of his family's hostility and for Ellice as, obviously, a scarlet woman.

Fortunately, the New Guinea option offered itself and the new couple sailed off to be married there. What a happy outcome this turned out to be. Ellice thrived in New Guinea, as the wife of a young but quite senior officer, in a hugely active social scene, in the middle of which was, of course, a piano.

Australian colonial life took very much after the British equivalent, on which it was studiously modelled. Formal dress for formal dinners, lots of staff, plenty of in-house entertaining and yes, the piano. Ellice was in seventh heaven. Wau was great, but Rabaul was better still. It offered a beautiful house on the rim of the volcano, a large colonial community and lots of social activity. There were even trips across to the Netherlands East Indies for Norm to visit the volcanoes there. People (planter colonists, scientists, administration officials and local Australian businessmen) came from all around Rabaul to hear Ellice play, and more importantly to take part in those friendly social evenings where everyone stood around the piano and sang. The piano, a grand no less, had made it up to New Guinea in the faithful, if ill-fated Burns Philp steamship Macdui, up the mountain to Wau, and finally across to Rabaul, quite a feat. This idyllic life lasted until 1942.

By that stage, Rabaul also figured in Japan's plans for military expansion, offering as it does one of the world's great harbours. After Pearl Harbour, it became clear that Japan would soon be coming south to invade New Guinea, and specifically to attack Rabaul. Clear not to everyone however, Norm firmly believing that all this military talk was nonsense. So, when the Australian Administration decided to evacuate all women and children from the Mandated Territory, Ellice was not on the boat. She had indeed the distinction of being the last white woman in the Territory. And, as such, a problem for the administration in distant Port Moresby.

As the Japanese advance moved ever more rapidly south, even Norm was persuaded that action had to be taken: a civil plane was despatched to Rabaul for the final staff evacuation, and Ellice was put on it. That was indeed the last non-military plane out of the Mandated Territory. As Ellice told it, the plane stopped en route at Salamaua, the port for the goldfields, where the airstrip was littered with gold bars which had had to be left behind by the fleeing mining community. They were, unfortunately, too heavy to fit into this last plane—despite the Captain's heroic efforts to try. The Japanese troops arriving later no doubt appreciated them greatly.

Ellice and Norm in Sydney circa 1946

Norm, however, true to his scepticism of all things military, did not take that last flight out. He joined the quaintly named and even more quaintly armed New Guinea Volunteer Rifles. They set up a gun emplacement on the front lawn of his lovely house with its magnificent view of the whole harbour and its approaches, and waited for the Japanese, who were not long coming. Indeed, in only a matter of days, in the early morning light the huge fleet of the invading Japanese Navy became more visible minute by minute, quickly followed by the arrival of the bombers. When the boats began landing the large Japanese invasion force immediately below them, the few Australians of the NG Volunteer Rifles were told that all hope was lost, every man for himself. Norm waited until the Japanese troops were within sight, coming up the road, and then set off on what became an epic escape across New Britain and thence in a very small fishing boat to Port Moresby—but that is another story. Needless to say, he was out of all contact for a very long time, and even after arriving in Port Moresby was hospitalised for many weeks with Blackwater fever.

Ellice meanwhile had been evacuated to Brisbane. That was a merciful relief—a reunion with daughter Lorelee, who had had to stay behind in Brisbane due to the absence of schooling in New Guinea, and—perhaps—far enough away from the hostile family.

Without any funds, and no doubt regretting those gold bars in Salamaua, she had to fend for herself. She took a job with the US Army, driving generals' cars. She was a dreadful driver, only recently having discovered that the brake could be used to slow down and not just to come to a sudden dead halt. After threatening the lives of several generals, the US Army put her through a driving course, after which she was much less of a menace on the roads.

With all that, she survived quite well, though without any news of Norm. No communications to the outside world were allowed by the Army authorities in Port Moresby, where Norm had arrived and been hospitalised for many months with Blackwater fever (extreme malaria). Finally, Ellice received via the Army a laconic and inaccurate message 'Happy Birthday, Norm'. At least she knew he was alive.

He finally made it down to Brisbane, hospitalised, and underwent a slow recovery. He had however come to the notice of General Macarthur's staff as one of the very few Australians who knew the geography and physical conditions of New Guinea well. On release from hospital, he went straight to work for the US Army on the preparations for the New Guinea campaign. Once well, Norm's and Ellice's life in Brisbane became both productive and civilised, given the circumstances.

With 1945 and the war over, another change of fate. The Chifley government threw itself not just into post-war reconstruction but into a whole new degree of nation-building for Australia. Some of the country's best and brightest came up with a plethora of ideas to make over and develop the country, buoyed with the optimism of victory in war and great hope for the future. The expansion—indeed even the discovery—of Australia's mineral wealth was a clear target. Norm's work with the US Army and his respected background in geological exploration of New Guinea came to the attention of the Chifley government, and Norm was duly asked to move to Canberra to become Chief Geologist of the new Bureau of Mineral Resources, tasked with the mapping and opening up of the continent, many parts of which had not at that time even been explored.

Canberra in the 1940s was something of a challenge to many transplants; but not if your reference point was colonial New Guinea. Canberra indeed at that time, though small, contained an extraordinary proportion of highly educated, highly motivated and highly intelligent professionals, brought in to work together to build the new Australia. With the creation of the ANU, this cohort grew even stronger. These were indeed pioneering days. Unfortunately, the availability of social distraction and entertainment was equally pioneering (and would remain so for many years). Norm and Ellice were very lucky. They bought a house with a very large garden, on National Circuit almost opposite the Prime Minister's Lodge. Norm, being at heart a country boy and thus used to doing everything himself, immediately set out to build a tennis court. He did this shovel load by shovel load, into the wheelbarrow, across the road and dumped in the Prime Minister's garden. When you are next invited to the Lodge, note the strawberry garden, sitting up proudly as it does: it is the product of the earth dug out from Norm's tennis court. Menzies, fortunately, approved.

The tennis court was a great boon for young Canberra society. So was daughter, Lorelee, now in her late teens and strikingly attractive. Given that, so many of the young pioneers who came to Canberra to shape the new country were still unmarried, the tennis court was a centre of fun and leisure, in a place where there was not much of that around. And, once again, in the middle, Ellice and the piano.

Just like in the old days of country Queensland, weekends in Canberra for many revolved around tennis afternoons, barbeque and singing around the piano in the evenings. Norm added to the attraction by digging out a swimming pool, the first private one in Canberra, again shovel by shovel load, and again across the road into the Menzies' garden, now some feet higher than before.

The late 1940s were therefore quite fun in emerging Canberra, even if in rather straightened circumstances, and the beginnings of the 1950s no less so for Ellice and Norm—thanks to daughter Lorelee who by that stage was becoming fully grown up and into the social whirl of the day. Lorelee was young, very attractive and highly vivacious—and most importantly, a single girl in Canberra where such were in short supply. Boys of much the same age were not in such short supply, including the Duntroon cadets, the new ANU students, diplomatic cadets from External Affairs, the Forestry School and the boys-on-the-land in the surrounding properties.

Once again, almost without a hiatus, the house in National Circuit was a social centre with its tennis, barbeques and late-night parties. As a small boy, it seemed to me that my sister's life consisted mainly of a series of balls, and decorating the Albert Hall as one of life's essential skills. Lorelee enrolled at University College (forerunner to ANU), did a brief flirtation with study concentrating, Norm drily observed, on social affairs. Finally, Lorelee married a Duntroon cadet, John Hooper, and left for married life in Melbourne.

Ellice clearly found that life rather lost its zim after that for a while. And perhaps, so did Norm. So, in 1954, he embarked on a remarkable change of pace by taking up an appointment with the UN to Bolivia. The year and a half in Bolivia plus six months each way at UN headquarters in New York meant a two-year absence from Canberra. The Australian government was not keen to let him go, so he actually resigned to take up the post, apparently sure that he would be welcomed back on his return (which indeed did turn out to be the case).

Bolivia was an extraordinary experience for Ellice. It was a country still really in the 19th century. Serfdom was still practiced, revolutions occurred on average every nine months, and it was as far from Australia as the globe allowed. It had just had a socialist revolution; the foreign capitalist mine owners had been thrown out and the mines nationalised; and the mines were not therefore doing well, since the incoming revolutionaries, although well motivated, were not much good in mine management. The UN, in those days very much under the influence of Scandinavian progressives, stepped in and sought to help the new Bolivian government to get the mines going again. Hence the request to Norm to come. La Paz, at 4000 metres high, is not an easy place to live at the best of times. Altitude sickness is inevitable, but at least temporary. Not so easy were the living conditions or availability of normal supplies. Norm found a lovely house, on the main thoroughfare. Ellice was disconcerted to note that all the front windows had bullet holes through them. She asked the agent about fixing them but the agent dismissed this request saying that there was no point repairing them, as they would only be shot up again in the next revolution.

Ellice found ways to make a very pleasant home in these unusual circumstances. The (very small) international community, mainly UN people, were very welcoming, and as Australians, the locals did not associate us with either the rapacious Americans or the brutal Spanish. Indeed, Bolivia was still in the throes of the particularly nasty form of Spanish colonialism where all profits went to the small Spanish ruling class and nothing at all was left to the indigenous population. One of Norm's early acts in La Paz was to free the serfs who came indentured with the house we rented. And to pay them an actual salary. This act caused waves, but the new government was delighted and we were invited to local events all over Bolivia. Norm was away a lot, the mines being located around the country and, as so often in the past, Ellice coped with maintaining the semblance of a normal life. She had of course the domestic staff (no English, needless to say), now delighted to be free, but a dreadful cook is still a dreadful cook. Meals were always formal, in the Spanish style, and always awful. We spent a lot of energy being polite to the chef, Gustavo, and trying not to let him see how ghastly his meals were, he being so proud of them. I hope he never found out that after struggling through another of his horrors, we would repair upstairs to the bedroom, lock the door and secretly toast bread on the one-bar radiator. The next half hour would be spent trying to wave the toast smell out the window so that Gustavo wouldn't be offended.

In fact, no revolution took place for the time we were there—a record—showing the popular strength of the revolution, whose descendants are indeed still in power today.

In contrast, the New York sojourns on the way there and back were great pressure relief opportunities. Ellice devoted herself to combat shopping in a way she never did before or since.

And so, back to Canberra, with a large sense of relief and welcome. As the 50s wore on, the excitement of early Canberra, or at least its pioneering spirit, faded, and with that the social and mothering role of wives of senior officers too. The house on National Circuit was still a beacon for tennis parties on weekends and, more importantly for Ellice, for the Tuesday mornings 'girls group' of close and similarly inclined old friends. Ellice was never a good tennis player, being short and not a natural athlete, but she made up for it by placing herself strategically at the net, from where she had at least a random chance of hitting the ball back with purpose.

But something was clearly lacking: a job was out of the question as Norm would never approve. Fortunately, something else came up. Ellice met in the late 1950s a Latvian refugee, Mme Lans, who had fled the Soviet Union but had earlier been with the Russian State Opera. Mme Lans's focus was on singers rather than pianists; she was classically trained in the unforgiving tradition of the Russian state institutions and she was keen to spread her knowledge in her new homeland. Ellice became a disciple, soaking up this wonderful source of expertise, and she soon set about imparting it to others by instructing students of her own. This was not the world of chorusing around the piano after dinner with drinks in hand, this was serious stuff. Ellice quickly became the go-to teacher in Canberra for anyone seeking a singing career. It came to include frequent public appearances in concert, in competition and on the ABC as an accompanist. By the late 1960s, she was well-known in musical circles around the country.

She also took fees for her services. These were pretty haphazardly arranged affairs, she being most reluctant to ever raise or discuss money, and Norm was not really comfortable with the whole idea of her 'working'. But take money she did, and quickly became rather taken with the results. She bought a new(ish) car 'with her own money', and from then on, claimed most domestic purchases as her own contribution. Norm played along, rather preoccupied with this own workload as Director of the Bureau of Mineral Resources (now called Geoscience Australia) at a time of huge successes in mineral discoveries around Australia. The 1960s were a period of normality. I was growing up through school and university. Norm occupied his spare time by building a beach house in Dalmeny on the NSW south coast. I was a swimmer and a surfer, so this house was ostensibly for me but in fact, it was mainly because he wanted to build a house. As earlier with pool and tennis court in Canberra, he did indeed build the house entirely by himself. No tradesman ever participated except an electrician (a legal requirement). To make it more challenging, he made it an A-frame house, so that as he put it, he could have the fun of working on the basis of 22.5 degree—not 90 degree—angles. The house remained for many years and was well used as a party place for various friends and families. The locals thought it extraordinary, believing it really ought to have been a church.

In the mid-1960s, Norm decided once again that it was time for a change, and he took up another UN offer, this time to Israel. Ellice was less enthusiastic about this posting, even though it was only six months long. She found living in Jerusalem difficult and unwelcoming—certainly, Tel Aviv would have been much more congenial. And I think she was quite homesick for Canberra.

By the late 1960s, I had graduated from University and got a job with the (then) Department of External Affairs as a diplomatic cadet. More importantly, I married Kerry, who made up for some of my own failings in at least Norm's eyes: firstly, she was a Science graduate, a course which I had refused to do despite Norm's urgent prodding, and secondly because she was good at tennis.

Norm retired in 1975, and was elected President of the World Geological Congress. This involved a great deal of international travel, which Ellice loved, and especially to China, since Norm had been instrumental in getting China admitted to the World Congress, an achievement which the Chinese never forgot. Their visits to China therefore were rather magnificent affairs, and Ellice certainly loved that too.

From the 1970s, life was quieter. Norm was still preoccupied with his tennis, which indeed he continued to play almost until his own death at 98. For Ellice, eventually the piano did fall silent. Quite suddenly, after a brief illness, and therefore not practising at all for a while, she felt she had 'lost' her touch. She gave up playing almost immediately rather than go slowly downhill. Sadly, it was thc bcginning of a long downhill, not just on the piano.

Chapter 5

Marjorie Moffat Hinchliffe (Née Smyth)

Meredith Hinchliffe

Murr and I first met when she commenced boarding at CCEGGS in 1960. Murr was very creative which was fortunate as it turned out. She suffered terribly from chilblains during the cold Canberra weather. As a result, she knitted an extraordinary nose protector adorned with a pompom. Coloured green to go with the school uniform, it attached to her ears and covered her nose. I am not sure how well it worked but it created a lot of interest. We were 14 years old and impressionable. Being her friend was not an option. Murr had amazing stories to tell especially about boys. Over the years and our parallel interests in things Sydney, the ALP and the Woman's Electoral Lobby. I saw a lot of Murr and her mother at her home in Chatswood. She was a fabulous cook and, like her daughter, full of fascinating stories of her journeys all over the world.

Robbie Henderson

Marjorie Moffat Smyth was born on either April 11 or April 12, 1920 in Warwick, Queensland. The family was always uncertain about the date, as her father reportedly forgot it when he registered her birth. Her father, John Sands Smyth, was a general practitioner in Warwick.

He had enlisted as a medical practitioner in World War I when he was 30 years old and was a Major in the 9th Australian Field Ambulance. He was married to Nellie Beatrice Crouch and they had three daughters, the middle one being my mother. Her family came from Orange and his was in Sydney.

The three girls were sent to board at non-denominational Ascham School, Edgecliff in the eastern suburbs, Sydney.

When she left school, my mother, Marjorie, undertook accounting qualifications and worked at what later became Coopers and Lybrand. She lived in a flat in Elizabeth Bay with sisters Rosemary and Ruth Dobson. Rosemary, who became a highly respected poet, was my godmother and Ruth, Australia's first female ambassador.

Marjorie as a young woman

During the war, Marjorie left the accounting firm and went to work in the signals directorate at the Royal Australian Navy base at Garden Island. It was here that she met my father, Leslie Maxwell Hinchliffe (Max).

He was a Lieutenant Commander when they were married on August 18, 1945. Family history has it that he and his groomsman travelled from Sydney to Warwick by train, two days after the end of World War II. During the trip, they filled condoms with water and threw them out at the stations when they stopped.

Max was an anti-submariner, and was awarded a Distinguished Service Cross in his role as beach master for the evacuation of troops at the Battle of Crete on the nights of 28/29 and 30/31 May 1941. He survived being sunk in a Canadian ship in 1943 on his return to England.

It appears that Marjorie continued working until she became pregnant. I was born on September 7, 1946 and my brother Jonathan Maxwell on February 27, 1948. At the time, we lived in Bellevue Hill, Sydney. In the early 1950s, my parents bought a house in Chatswood in Sydney.

Marjorie as a young mother

My mother spent nine months in Royal North Shore Hospital with nephritis not long after they bought the house, and we believe she was one of the first people to survive this debilitating disease. Jonathan and I were sent to various relatives around NSW during this difficult time.

It would have been difficult for my mother to have continued to work, even if she had wanted to do so; her life was subjugated by Max' occupation. We moved every two years or so, and she made a comfortable home in each city.

In 1955–56, Max was appointed to the Navy Office in Melbourne. We swapped houses with a family who had been appointed to a job in Sydney. My mother became pregnant again, but due to the nephritis, she had to have a termination, as the risk to her life was too high.

In 1957, my father was appointed Staff Officer to the Head of Australian Joint Services Staff, Washington DC and the family travelled by the P & O ocean liner Orion to Vancouver, Canada and then by train across the continent through the Rocky Mountains to New York City. We lived in Washington for two years and travelled all over the country.

Marjorie and Max at Harman circa 1959

Max's diplomatic job involved an extraordinary amount of entertaining, both attending and giving cocktail and dinner parties. Marjorie's weekly letters to her parents described the parties and in one period of ten days, she gave details of numerous parties. Unfortunately, as she was always troubled by excess weight, continuous eating and drinking was always a problem for my mother.

She was an excellent dressmaker and made all her clothes for these parties, and all of mine. She also made my brother's school clothes until he started wearing long pants.

They returned to Australia in 1959, when Max became the Commanding Officer of HMAS Harman in Canberra. We lived there until May 1960 when they travelled to Manus Island where he became Naval Officer in Charge Papua New Guinea. The weatherboard house we lived in at Harman was not the designated house for the CO, which had become the wardroom, so we lived in the executive officer's (EO's) designated house. It had three bedrooms and a separate dining room, but did not have wall-to-wall carpet. The EO was only entitled to a square of carpet in the middle of the sitting, dining and main bedrooms although the two smaller bedrooms had old carpet, perhaps installed by previous tenants.

The house had an open fireplace and a wood stove in the kitchen. It was very cold in winter, and probably hot in summer. Marjorie mastered the stove and we spent a great deal of time in the kitchen.

She was an excellent cook—and nearly always cooked for the parties in Washington and Harman. While the entertaining wasn't as demanding there, they had many friends in Canberra and had many dinners, and we went on many picnics.

When they moved to Manus Island, my mother continued the extensive letter writing to the family members and we are fortunate that my grandparents kept most of them. Despite it being quite isolated, there were always people travelling through Manus; Marjorie describes in detail the visits by military officers from Australia and the United States, various scientists, senior religious groups and of course my brother and me.

My parents often had people staying in the house, entertaining and arranging interesting activities for them. They were always determined that people saw the best of the island.

The government subsidised one visit a year for children from Sydney to PNG, and over the long Christmas holidays in 1960, there were over 2000 children travelling from Australia. Money was always an issue for the parents, as they had to pay our school fees and all the other costs associated with our being in Australia.

My mother's letters from Manus describe a very interesting life on this small island. She became involved in the local pre-school committee, acting as treasurer and raising funds for equipment. There were six staff in the house known as haus bois, and she came to grips with dealing with them quite quickly. She was disappointed that they were required to speak English, as she had been looking forward to learning to speak pidgin. Early into her time there, they had to move the cook boi on and she trained the boi who had had formerly done the housework. She commented that like her, he loved cooking and disliked housework. He became a very good cook.

They went on many picnics, and both Max and Marjorie became interested in collecting shells and she loved nothing better than walking across the reefs in her ankle high waterproof boots watching the fish, or lying on her tummy looking through a glass-bottomed box, watching the fish and other aquatic life on the reefs.

Max and Marjorie stayed on Manus for just under two years. My brother and I visited only twice, the second time in the September holidays. We were 16 and 14 respectively and we both took friends with us on the second trip. The letters report that we spent a great deal of the time in our bedrooms, playing records. In reality, our parents went out of their way to ensure that we all had fun and an interesting time. We played tennis—which Marjorie had taken up again—and badminton and the boys went fishing, and we went on lots of picnics. We both remember our time on Manus very fondly. My mother's letters record the last week of frantic washing, making clothes for me, mending them for Jonathan and finding things which we hadn't used since we had arrived.

Max was appointed Chief Staff Officer to the Flag Officer Commanding the Eastern Area of Australia at the end of 1962 and they returned to Sydney just before Christmas. They took up residence in a lovely, big, upstairs flat in a block owned by the Navy just above Garden Island. Jonathan and I stayed at boarding school until our schooling finished—1963 for me and 1964 for Jonathan.

Max was due to be invalided out of the Navy in March 1964 but was asked to remain in his position following the HMAS Melbourne/HMAS Voyager collision. Marjorie rallied around and visited many of the wives of the injured and deceased sailors. She was always a tower of strength for these women, who often had very little education and relied on their husbands for everything. She was horrified one day when she visited a young wife who hadn't had any money for over a week and when she inquired about the cheque that had been sent, the woman replied that she didn't know what it was and she had put it in a drawer.

In perhaps June 1964, they moved back to their house in Chatswood, where they had not lived in since 1953. It was very run down and they undertook some renovations. I was living at home at the time and it was difficult moving all our possessions into a much smaller house.

I am sure Marjorie missed the interesting life she had lived in Washington DC, Manus and then in Potts Point, but she settled into being a housewife, still holding cocktail and dinner parties. She gave me a pair of stockings as a bribe to help clear the table and do the washing up.

Marjorie worked in various charities, including the Royal North Shore Hospital Women's Auxiliary where she was treasurer, and the Royal Far West Children's home in Manly, where she was also treasurer. She was disappointed when she found that she was unable to translate books into brail on a special machine.

I will always remember how carefully she planned the week's meals for the family, never having the same meat twice in a row and never having a similar meal. If we had a grill one night, the next it would be a casserole.

We never worked well together in the kitchen except when we made the Christmas pudding, a role we took over from my grandparents when we returned to Sydney. I still make the Christmas pudding and cake using her great-grandmother's recipes.

Marjorie was quite conservative. She could not understand why I was involved in feminism and accused me of 'just waiting around' for the right man to come along. She also did not understand my interest in Labor politics. When the man who became my husband moved in with me in Canberra, she told me that she would not visit us at the house—which she owned. That lasted about eighteen months and then, of course, they stayed with us occasionally.

Marjorie in later life

Marjorie had her first stroke in 1978, three months after we were married. She never really recovered, and continued having smaller strokes and began drifting into dementia. When Max had a heart attack, she had to move to respite care and eventually, we all realised that he could no longer look after her at home. He had been her carer and nursed her for twenty years. He visited her regularly in the nursing home, helping her, caring for her without any meaningful response for the final five years of her life. We found many letters from him to her, expressing his love and devotion.

Marjorie Hinchliffe died on 10 August 1998.

Chapter 6

Jean Gulson (Née Robertson)

Kerry Fisher

Kerry and I met as contemporaries in the science faculty at ANU in 1964. She was a very happy and conscientious science student. Living in Bruce Hall, she soon became friends with the group from CCEGGS and CGS, especially Bill Fisher, who was to become her life partner.

The Gulson brickworks were the first indication we had reached Goulburn on the way back to Canberra from Sydney. We had many trips to Goulburn to attend various balls and events and Kerry's mother Jean always welcomed us to the house on the hill facing the brickworks. After finishing her degree, Kerry attended teacher's college in Sydney before commencing her interesting life as a diplomat's partner.

Robbie Henderson

My mother, Jean, was the middle of three girls. She lived all her life—before meeting Dad—in Tasmania, at Rosetta and later Glenorchy, both in those days on the outskirts of Hobart. She left school to work at 14 years old, during the Great Depression, so that her elder sister could continue studying to become a schoolteacher. Being the Depression, the family needed as much money as they could earn to put food on the table.

Mum's was a very Scottish family and Presbyterian to the hilt. Her father was a Scottish immigrant, and ran a typical Scottish household. Her own mother however, was Tasmania-born, and for all her life, and most of ours, we all believed the family story that they were free settlers who had been there for three generations.

Imagine our surprise, and perhaps glee, to find out recently that they (the original settlers, her grandparents) had come to Australia as convicts. A fact they definitely would not have shared with anyone. I imagine very many Australian families have a similar story, if only they knew about it. Only one of the three sisters ever knew.

During the war, Jean worked in the Cadbury's Chocolate Factory at Claremont, outside Hobart, Tasmania, close to where she lived and had grown up. She was placed in the export division, which was important for Australia as chocolate was sent to the soldiers overseas. It was considered an even more vital contribution to the war effort than joining the WAAF as it turned out.

Mum had a fiancé who was in the RAAF who was killed early in the war. Mum never spoke about him and I never asked her about him. It must have happened very early in the piece. Later she met my father (also in the RAAF—a wireless air gunner on the Catalina flying boats).

Mum applied for, and was accepted, to join the WAAFs but her boss in Cadburys 'manpowered' her, saying she was too valuable to go in the women's Air Force and he needed her doing exactly what she was doing for the war effort, distributing chocolates. She stayed at Cadbury's until she married Dad in October 1943.

Dad managed to get a couple of 'leave rides' to Hobart with the RAAF during the war, as he also had relatives in Hobart whom he was authorised to visit. Happily, his relatives knew my mother—and that is how the two of them met.

After their marriage in Glenorchy, in 1943, Mum left Cadburys. She and Dad went to live on the mainland. This was considered a huge move at the time, leaving hearth and home behind in Tasmania for a totally new environment. Unable to work, she lived with a family of a doctor in Melbourne minding their three children. Mum loved children and was happy to mind them, especially as Dad was gone with the RAAF much of the time.

Then they were posted to Rathmines Air Force Base (on Lake Macquarie near Newcastle). We children are still in touch with some of the people they met and knew there, and their children too. They are some of our closest friends even to this day.

My parents' 60th wedding anniversary

I suppose Mum was always worried that Dad wouldn't return one day. Luckily, Dad was released from the RAAF quickly at the end of the war. His father had a brickwork in Goulburn NSW, and I guess the authorities knew they would need houses for folk who had married during the war years.

So, Dad and Mum moved to Goulburn, where I was born in September 1946. We lived with Dad's sister and her husband (and his elderly father) for three years until we moved into our own home nearby, in Goulburn, in 1948.

Mum seemed to like being a mother after her working days in Hobart, as she had always loved children. My two sisters arrived in 1949 and 1953, so she soon had her hands full with the three of us. I never heard her grumble about missing her life before marriage; I think they were all glad the war was over. It ruined so many years of so many people's lives.

Despite being busy raising children, Jean managed to have an active social life, revolving especially around the church (Presbyterian later Uniting (UCA)) and the Goulburn Golf Club, especially after we children had gone to school. She became Captain of the women's golf team, and played for many years all around the district. She was very pleased to get her handicap down to 12! She was still playing golf until she was diagnosed with cancer at 82.

In later life, after Dad's retirement, they moved to the NSW south coast, having found a lovely house right on the beach in Narrawallee (Ulladulla). It had three quite large guest bedrooms, enough for all three daughters and their own families to come and stay at the same time—as it turned out a total of 13. I thought Mum was so happy during these family visits reviving her immediate family ties, this time in the role of a matriarch.

Mum was very proud of her three girls. She did everything to see that our lives were better than the one she had had. She was especially happy when we each graduated from university (ANU in Canberra)—quite an achievement for a family with no previous experience or expectation of tertiary studies.

Looking back, I realise that Mum gave up so much for her family—her own sisters as well as her children. Had she grown-up in the post-war world, she would have had so many opportunities, which were just not available back then.

Chapter 7

Laurel Elise Constance Henderson (Née Sutton)

Robbie Henderson

My mother, Laurel Elise Constance Sutton, was born on 12 December 1916 at Manildra, NSW. She died on 25 July 2012. She was the second child and second daughter of Arthur John Sutton (Pop) and Ella Mary Myrtle Ridley. He was a baker and she, a 'homemaker' and vigorous gardener. People tell me that my grandmother thought she would marry a farmer. Whether that was true or not, she seemed to be happy with Pop. The Forbes Advocate, 19 September 1913 described their wedding as elaborate; in a church full of flowers and a full choral service; a sign of things to come for my mother who inherited both the love of flowers and music.

My grandfather was a teetotaller and a very strict Protestant. By all accounts, he was an excellent baker, he won many awards. According to the National Advocate 23 November 1934, 'the well-known firm of Sutton Bros Bakers of Bathurst secured first prize in the country section, open to all country bakers of the State of NSW and third prize in the city and country combined section. They also secured the Champion Cup awarded to the baker securing the greatest aggregate of points in the country zone'. Pop was a member of 'the Orange Lodge' and its principles guided his life.

After he sold the business on retirement, he and my grandmother moved to Queanbeyan to live with my parents. My grandmother died when I was three after which Pop spent six months of the year living with each of his daughters until he died in Canberra at the age of 92. He was a great supporter of girls' education and the importance of the three 'R's' as he put it, a fact that benefitted Mum and her sister, and later my sister and me.

After living initially in Rankin Street, the Suttons moved to a beautiful federation house called Kennington in William St, Bathurst. It had huge grounds full of flowers, a ballroom and numerous bedrooms. My grandmother bought it with her inheritance. I remember thinking it was odd that we all knew this and I have wondered since whether it was just a continual reminder of the farming connection. Grandma was certainly proud of her Ridley heritage, as was my mother.

The house is still standing, although a substantial part of the grounds has been sold off over the years. The house was designed in 1906 by architect J.J. Copeman. John Copeman also designed the School of Arts at Rockley, NSW. Coincidently, my parents went to live there when they were first married.

Kennington was very important to my mother. Probably, her time spent there was the happiest part of her life and she often yearned for it. When she was very old, she talked of it constantly. It was her rock; a place where she was secure.

'Kennington' Bathurst circa 1942

My grandmother, who suffered from frequent illnesses, was a hardworking and busy woman and an excellent cook. With small boys to look after and a large house to care for, I am not sure how much of her attention my mother received. Somehow, I think it was less than she would have liked. Maybe my mother was a bit too cheerful and a bit of a show off; who knows, she certainly respected her mother and all her competencies.

Always called Mother by Mum and my aunt, I think Grandma Sutton may have been a bit harder on her daughters than she was on her sons, although my memory of her was of a kind and friendly woman.

Mum, or Mimsie, as I called her, was one of four children. Her sister, Enid, was two years older and her brothers Ralph and Winston several years younger. Mum and Enid were very close friends and remained so for the whole of their lives.

By all accounts, the family was very happy at Kennington. Sometimes, my grandmother took in boarders to supplement the family's income. She also sold flowers to the Flemington markets in Sydney getting up early so she could put them on the train to arrive in time for sale. Childhood in Bathurst NSW seemed magical to me. My mother's stories were elaborate and full of richness.

Laurel and Bill at a fancy-dress ball in Sydney in the late 1930s

In accordance with the traditions of the time, my mother was brought up to be a 'lady'. She was taught piano from an early age. She told of how she and her sister were sent off to lessons in the dark in the freezing cold of Bathurst early winter mornings and had to put their fingers into bowls of hot water before they could work the keys. She must have worked them hard for the National Advocate (Bathurst NSW) 17 December 1932 noted that Laurel Sutton had won a special prize for good work in her music examinations. She subsequently won a number of these prizes and progressed through all her grades for Trinity College London, which was the first organisation to offer examinations in music to external students in Australia, starting in 1877. Mum often talked of the cap and the black bachelors' gown with violet and purple silk hood she was entitled to, but as far as I know, she did not own one.

My parents' wedding in Bathurst 23 August 1941

My mother and Enid attended Pixie Ladies College, Bathurst where Miss Ross was their much-respected headmistress. Apparently, my mother was so sad when her sister, started school that Miss Ross let her attend at an early age, so she did not feel left out. A press clipping from the Bathurst Free Press and Mining Journal, 28 September 1901 noted that 'the girls of Pixie were taught to be strong, self-controlled, and, above all, good women'—such were my mother and aunt. They were taught French at an early age and Mum could remember her French vocab when she was well into her 90s.

The Methodist church was my mother's social and spiritual life. She was also a keen Brownie, Guide and Rover and gardener of course.

Mum left school having completed her NSW Intermediate Certificate. She wanted to become a florist but this did not eventuate. Instead, she became a governess and music teacher to small children on a large property in the Central West of New South Wales; a job she enjoyed as it enabled her to indulge her passion for horse-riding. One story my father told me was how, having ridden her horse into a barbwire fence and cutting her leg badly, Mum, concerned she might be prevented from riding for a while, took a rabbit from a trap and placed it over her leg so her employers would think it was the rabbit, and not she, who was bleeding.

Laurel Sutton circa 1935

My mother and father met in Nowra, NSW when my two grandfathers, both bakers, appeared to have worked together for a short period. At the time, Mum was courting a local farmer, but my father's suit prevailed and they married in Bathurst on 23 August 1941.

Their wedding was very similar to that of my grandmother's. According to the local paper, the breakfast was held at Kennington where 'the reception room was decorated with daffodils and sweet peas. The tables were decorated with pink stock and carnations, pride of place being given a three-decker diamond shape wedding cake, decorated in delicate pink and fancy ornaments, the work of the bridegroom. The church and supper room were decorated with silver fern, pink stock and silver bells and silver luck shoes, by friends of the bride and bridegroom'.

Despite being an excellent cake decorator, my father reluctantly followed the family tradition of becoming a baker; an MB as he jokingly called himself. The only thing he seemed to like about it was being his own boss, a bad thing given he was a hopeless businessman who rarely collected debts owed to him; spending when he had money and forgetting to pay the taxman, much to my mother's horror. This unfortunate practice continued to be the source of many battles throughout their married life.

They moved to the little town of Rockley NSW nestled beside Peppers Creek, where my father opened a bakery and shop and they lived in part of the local School of Arts. Their time there was to be very short as my father had enlisted on 16 September 1939 and by the end of 1941, he was serving in the Australian Army in Borneo and Papua New Guinea in World War 2 where he joined the Intelligence Service. My sister was born on the 23 September 1942.

My Aunt Enid's husband had also enlisted. She had a small son by the time my uncle went to the war. Both Enid and Mum went back to live with their parents and their small children in their childhood home, Kennington for the remainder of the war. With built-in childcare, Enid and Laurel were free to become auxiliary members of the Women's Land Army formed in 1942. They worked hard contributing to the war effort mowing hay, picking vegetables and packing trucks. Probably, for the first time in their lives, they received a guaranteed income as army wives and operated quite independently of their husbands.

It may sound heartless to say that both women had a good war, but I think they did. In fact, they were probably very happy enjoying one another's company and that of their little children in a relatively safe and free environment. All that changed with the end of the war when they left Kennington for ever and the reality of peace and married life, in somewhat straightened circumstances, set in.

Finding some letters that my mother wrote to my father shortly after he had returned from Borneo and had preceded her to Queanbeyan to establish a business, made me wonder how constrained her life had become post war. The letters are tentative and polite as if written by a stranger. Much of the text consists of requests for permission to spend money on domestic purchases. Unfortunately, Dad's responses have not been preserved but he must have found these missives strange. Difficult too was his relationship with my sister. Like so many other fathers, Dad had come home to a child who did not know him and who resented his presence and the time he spent with her mother. Sadly, his father/child relationship was permanently affected and my mother was compromised in the process.

I was born in January 1947, while Mum was still in Bathurst. My father and I were close friends always and I have often wondered if it had not been for the war, whether our family relations would have been different. As it turned out, throughout my childhood and early adulthood, my sister was my mother's closest companion and I was Dad's.

The letters from my mother to my father contained a passionate plea for her parents to be allowed to come and live with them and for Pop to help Dad in the business. It seems an odd request today, but even if my father had preferred to restart his marriage in close family relationship, it was not to be and my grandparents became part of an extended family life.

Life in Queanbeyan was difficult for Mum. Going to church was an important part of her social life, especially as it involved two of her great passions—music and flowers. These pleasures sustained her while she lived there. She also played tennis and bowls and had afternoon tea parties; we all sang around the piano, but it was not like Bathurst.

As a centre of post war migration, the town was often unfairly referred to as 'struggle town' and Mum did not feel a part of it. She entered willingly into helping to prepare for the 'by proxy marriages' conducted for my father's migrant workers over our telephone with their unknown wives to be in Malta, Italy and Serbia.

She collected the white and pink sugar almonds in little lace baskets and placed them around the phone, so it felt like an actual wedding. She also met these poor women at the boat and helped them to settle into their new home amongst people with whom they could not communicate and with husbands they had never met. She supported my father in his work with the Good Neighbour Council; but this did not fulfil her. My father was always busy with the business, engaging in some unknown intelligence activity or attending to some good cause or other and I think she was lonely.

Mum never learnt to drive, as she was constantly afraid of hitting someone but she loved to fly. I well remember accompanying her on my first trip on a plane when I was about four years old. My uncle, Ralph, was sent to Korea with the army and my mother and I went to see him, and the other troops, off to the war. I thought it was an adventure but it was clearly of great concern to Mum. We took boxes of goodies, designed to sustain life in the cold, which Mum and my aunts had prepared over many weeks. These consisted of knitted socks, gloves and fruitcake.

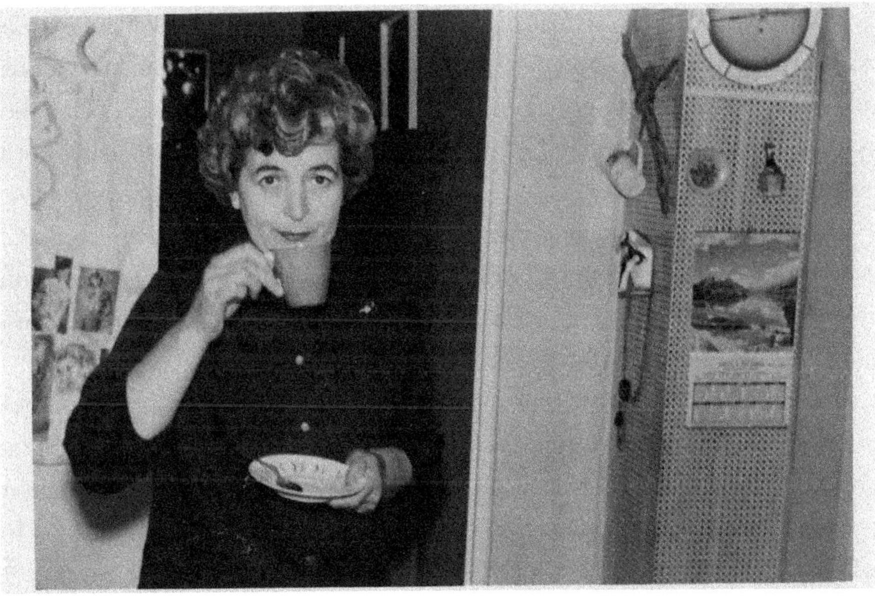

Great Grandma Laurel (GG) in the late 1990s

Mum was a dedicated mother and a great storyteller. Often when we were small, she would recite poetry to us when we were about to go to sleep. She was very expressive and sometimes the poems seemed scary.

It was a dark and stormy night and the billy goat was blind, he backed into a barbed wire fence and hurt his, never you mind!

One of her favourites was the Gypsy Man:

'Time, you old gypsy man why hasten away?
Because
Her mother said, she never should, play with the gypsies in the wood; If she did, her mother would say. You naughty girl to disobey'.

They were all somewhat odd.

We moved to Bowral when I was six years old ostensibly so my sister and I could attend Annesley School for Girls. It was a very nice place to live and my mother fitted in perfectly doing the things she loved best but my father did not come. He stayed with the business in Queanbeyan and we only saw him on occasional weekends or when he came to collect us to take as to someone's place or a boarding house for holidays. He could never stay for longer than a weekend and I do not remember ever having a proper holiday with him. Years later, both my parents told me that they had come close to separating permanently during this period.

In 1954, while my uncle Ralph was part of the Australian Army contingent on tour with the new young Queen Elizabeth II, my aunt, who had accompanied him, contracted polio whilst pregnant. It was a very dramatic event and caused an official stir given the contagious nature of the disease.

When the baby was born (my cousin John), he came to live with us in Bowral for several months while my aunt was in rehabilitation. Over the following years, my mother spent many months helping my aunt with her small children and my sister and I spent periods in boarding school whilst she did so. Over the next five years or so, we shuffled between Bowral and Queanbeyan until eventually my father sold the business and we all moved to Canberra permanently. In 1956, we commenced at the Canberra Church of England Girls Grammar Schools (CCEGGS) where we stayed until we completed our schooling.

Mum was much happier in Canberra than she had been in Queanbeyan probably because my father had left the business. With little money in the family coffers, Mum took up caring for children once more, teaching music and providing support for a disabled woman. With more time available to him, Dad attended the then Canberra University College, studying languages and political science.

Canberra was to be her home for the rest of my mother's life. For many years, the National Memorial Methodist Church in Forrest was the centre of her social life. She played the piano for the various activities conducted there and went painting with the 'ladies'.

In later years, she supported my sister and me through school and university; cared for our babies when we had them and became their ally and best friend as they grew up and started to challenge their mothers as we had her. They loved her and she loved them with a great generosity of spirit; she shared their interests and often their undertakings.

I often wondered whether my mother was happy. Despite a lack of money, she always dressed well, even gardening in her stockings in summer. She never complained and, while she held strong views about what was proper behaviour and had a very real commitment to social justice and Christian values, it was often difficult to work out what she was thinking.

We always knew we had to ensure our seams were straight and not to slouch. If we did something she did not like, she would send us 'to Coventry' for quite a few days, but she rarely said what she had on her mind. I was surprised once when she accused me of treating the house like a hotel and her like a servant. The real cause was actually because I always read at the breakfast table.

Mostly, our table was the scene of arguments about ideas and politics, especially between my grandfather, father and, as my sister and I grew up, us. Mum rarely contributed. In 1972, both she and my grandfather stopped supporting the Liberal Party and as we girls became more involved in the Women's Movement and political activity, she moved further to the left. She always said she was voting for the person but from 1975 onwards, she was a consistent Labor voter.

Did the war affect my mother's life and expectations? I think it did a great deal, as the charming debonair man she married was not the same man who came back from the battles. My father wanted to stay and work in the Pacific but my mother did not want to have to send her girls away to school. Between bouts of malaria and the many causes my father felt he had to fight I think Mum had to learn to compromise and accept that the certain life she had led as a child at Kennington was gone for ever.

In the end, I think my parents managed to have a successful marriage although much shorter than either had expected. Dad died when he was 73 years old leaving my mother a widow for over 25 years. When I was tidying up my mother's things after she had died, I found a poem she had cut out from some magazine entitled Destined to be Alone. It made me sad to think that might have been the way she saw her life. She always seemed to be surrounded by people; people who cared for her and she for them. Maybe deep down, she was lonely, or disappointed that she had had such a domestic existence.

I learned a lot about Mum in the three years she was bedridden before she died. She remained cheerful and joked with her friend, Freda, who visited her daily. They also talked about the war. Freda was in Germany where she was raped by a Russian soldier. I think for the first time in all those years, Mum saw the war from another perspective.

As she reached the end of her life, she asked constantly when she was going back to Kennington to see her mother. I think at the end, she thought she had.

Grandma Laurel in the early 2000s

Chapter 8

Eleanor Bellamy Delaney (Née Mackaness)

Donelle Wheeler

I met Nell when she came to CCEGGS as a boarder. We were 12 years old. I liked her because she was cheerful and had dimples, something I had long wanted for myself. Despite my being a daygirl, Nell and I became good friends. I remember in an Ancient History class, which we both enjoyed, working out that our mothers had been pregnant at the same time given the age of our sisters and us. It was pretty silly but we thought it hilarious and it became a special bond. Nell always had lovely clothes made by her clever and stylish mother who visited Canberra often. We saw quite a bit of one another between Sydney and Canberra and in the 1970s, Nell and I became feminist warriors together and subsequently strong Labor Party supporters. I was delighted when many years later, Nell's (and Pip Wheeler's) daughter Victoria came to work with me on a university placement. She was just as clever and cheerful as her mother and grandmother and I felt the generations merge.

Robbie Henderson

My mother was a very stylish woman, tall (5'10", the same height as her granddaughter, Victoria) and slender. She was never other than beautifully turned out (as we would say)—clothes, hair, makeup all immaculate. The house was similarly tended—wonderful, large flower arrangements in the entrance hall, more in the living room. Everything neat and tidy—beds made, carpets swept, washing-up and wiping-up done, everything put away.

I am sorry to have to report that this was all done by Mum alone. My sister, Denise, and I were waited on hand and foot. Denise's fiancé, Jim, was shocked when he first came to visit by how indulged we were. Very occasionally we'd be asked—by Dad—to wash up after tea. In Crookwell, the meals of the day were, in order, breakfast, dinner and tea. When we went to Sydney to stay with Mum's parents, we had 'dinner for tea'.

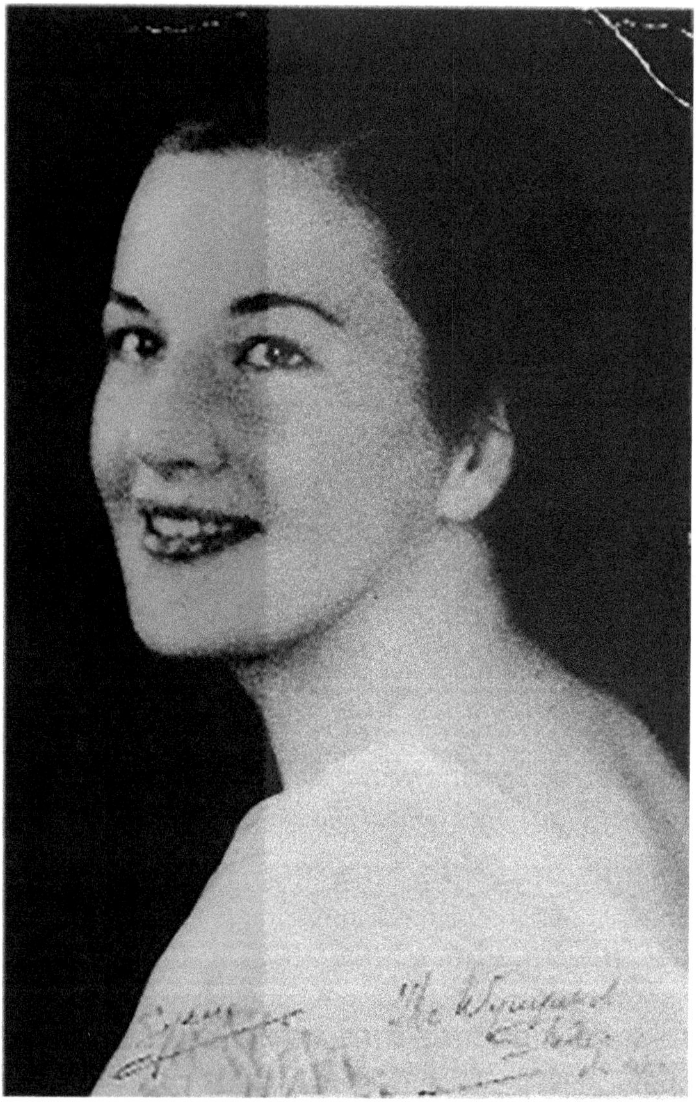

Eleanor aged 23 just prior to marrying

In Crookwell, Mum had loads of friends and lots to do. Her typical day started with a cup of tea in bed, made by Dad. Then she'd make a hot breakfast for everyone—she herself had only toast and marmalade with another cup of tea.

Then she'd plait my hair, dress me (yes, I didn't even do that until I went to boarding school) and send me off to school. Then she'd sit on a kitchen stool, light a cigarette and begin ringing her friends. Then there were the morning chores and the preparation of a hot dinner—which Dad and I would come home for—and in the afternoon, she would have friends around for afternoon tea (with home cooked slice—who could go past her Dutch ginger shortbread, known in our house later as 'Granny's regular'), go to visit them, play tennis, play cards, go to meetings of the Women's Hospital Auxiliary (she was the Secretary), get on with sewing something wonderful for herself or for us. Lots of her friends lived on properties out of town and she'd drive out for lunch or games of tennis—or whatever it was—and on those occasions Dad would have food left at home to heat up—or maybe it was sometimes sandwiches.

She was well-known among her friends as an extremely competent person. She taught many of them to drive. She had sat and passed her driving licence at the first opportunity and she drove confidently and well and fast! A nephew, driven by her to Crookwell from Sydney, was startled: he said when they arrived that he had known she drove fast, but hadn't realised that she was aiming to break the land speed record! She also taught many of her friends to sew and often helped them with sewing projects. She couldn't believe how difficult some people seemed to find things that she did with such flair and with such beautiful results.

Eleanor Delaney on her wedding day in December 1940

Her output was phenomenal. All soft furnishings in our house were made by her. She learnt how to make lampshades when I was about ten, so standard lamps and bedside lamps were all designed and produced by her from then on—and, when we were setting up our own homes, for Denise and me too. All her clothes, all Denise's clothes, all my clothes were made by her and then she made all our children clothes as well—and knitted their jumpers. She made clothes for special occasions for her mother. Famously, when she married, she made her dress, her bridesmaid's dress, her mother's dress and the cake. Then she repeated the trick for Denise's wedding and her grandson Michael's wedding as well, for which she made her dress, Denise's dress, my dress, Victoria's dress—and the cake! The curtains and bedspreads and chair coverings in our houses? Mum again. She had a spectacularly good eye for design and for colour and a great love of beautiful fabric.

She could draft a design from a photograph—or copy the design of a dress in a shop (which she did for Victoria for her end of Year 10 party). One memorable fabulous creation was copied from a Modess advertisement, which many of us will remember; it featured often in the Women's Weekly—a shimmering emerald green silk ball gown, fitted bodice, pinched in at the waist, with a very full skirt. Then she dyed her hair to match. Stunning. And a great thing to do with hair that had begun turning grey when she was 17 and was quite grey by the time I was born (when she was thirty). Green, I thought, vastly preferable to the blue rinse that later became fashionable. She did the matching gown and hair only one other time, this time pink.

Eleanor was the first-born child and only daughter of James Vincent Mackaness and Eleanor Frances Bellamy. Her father was the much loved, but defiant black sheep of the intellectual Mackaness family. His brother was a distinguished academic as were two of his sisters but James Vincent would row into the middle of the Parramatta River to avoid going to school, even though he was enrolled at Fort St Boys' High. And importantly, he did not encourage his daughter in other than the domestic arts, declaring that 'no daughter of his would work'. It would, he thought, reflect badly on him. Her brothers both went to university, one did Medicine, the other Engineering and all her cousins went to university too. Mum's brother said she wasn't a scholar, hated exams and I can imagine that is true, but then, that would not be surprising given the lack of encouragement from her father.

Eleanor was 22 years old at the outbreak of war and was living at home in Huntley's Point, a harbour side suburb of Sydney. She had already met Dad who also lived at home just a few blocks away. She had studied Domestic Science (dressmaking, tailoring, millinery and baking) at East Sydney Technical College and there she did excel. That had been encouraged at her home: her mother had come to rely on Eleanor for housework and for help in raising her two sons. She always turned her mother and brothers out immaculately and I believe she did a lot of the cooking in the house too.

She was spirited and energetic—rarely sitting still. She played tennis and went sailing with Dad when they were courting. And she withstood her brothers' merciless teasing and her father's outright opposition to her engagement to Dad. She was quick witted and she had a prodigious memory—her own mother was said by the family to have 'perfect recall'—and I don't think at her peak Mum was far from that pinnacle.

Her part in the war effort was as Voluntary Aid and as a Red Cross volunteer. She was also a Girl Guide and later became a Guide Commissioner. She contributed enthusiastically to 'Bundles for Britain' with small striped jumpers made from left-over wool, but she stopped when she saw one, she recognised that she'd made on a child in George St, obviously too attractive to be sent to Britain!

She and Dad married in December 1940 and went to live in the house she had been brought up in at Cheltenham, which they rented from her father. Dad was in the Army Reserve as he had been since early in the war. My sister, Denise, was born in March 1942 and Dad enlisted in the Army.

Mum was then living in Cheltenham by herself in her old family home with a small child. She had a very good friend, Dolly, who lived not far away and they saw a lot of one another and she knew a lot of people in the area, so I imagine that she was well supported. Remembering that she was brought up as a homemaker, I imagine there was a lot of sewing and knitting for the baby and a lot of curtain making, cushion covering and food preparation. She was not out of touch with Dad either. She visited him when he was posted in Brisbane and he did come home on leave.

She went by train every weekend with Denise to Huntley's Point to stay with her parents and her brothers. Denise was a much loved first grandchild and first niece and Mum adored her brothers who were funny and affectionate and just embarking on their own independent lives. Her brother, George, was engaged to Gwyn and Mum used to speak of wonderfully noisy and cheerful meals with the whole family and their friends—she would be shovelling food into Denise, her father would be reliving his bowls match with cutlery and condiment props, her brothers almost certainly engaged in arguments about the merits of one car or another, Gwyn usually with her head in a book and her mother presiding calmly over the lot. And although her father was self-centred, he did bring her a cup of tea every morning of her life as a young woman at home and when she visited as a married woman.

Her family was fortunate too in their war experience. Her brothers were at university and exempt from service and her husband and his three brothers all returned safely from the war.

There was upheaval though at the end of the war when Mum and Dad moved from all this warmth and comfort to the small cold township of Crookwell, four hours' drive from Sydney. There Dad was given the job of running the family business. Mum, we were told, agreed to this move on the grounds that it was only for one year. Forty years later, she and Dad moved back to Sydney, a second move she didn't like at all, since she had found life in Crookwell filled with friends in the town and friends on the land for whom she provided a contact point in the town. Dad, like her father, thought that it would reflect badly on him if she joined the paid workforce, but she didn't ever seem to want to do that, fulfilled by and excelling in the domestic sphere.

Life was pretty simple too. Every year when we were young, Dad would take his full three weeks annual leave and we would go to Dalmeny on the NSW South Coast where his step-cousin owned beach shacks which we'd rent—glorious holidays as I recall, Dad was never happier than when he was near the water. Both Denise and I were taught to surf by him and delighted in teasing our mother by challenging each other to a race to New Zealand, leaving her on the shore calling out, 'come back in, come back in'. Poor thing, I feel for her now, though I found it very amusing at the time! I think Dad may have done some cooking over these holidays, but I'm pretty sure Mum still did most of the housework.

She had a lot of funny sayings and played happily with words. She delighted in the local Crookwell lingo, so roads into private properties were always called 'get intos' (mostly 'bad get intos'), aches and pains blamed on 'the arthuritis'—and she laughed for days when the local paper referred to the sudden death of the hospital matron as having been caused by a 'coronary conclusion'! And we were brought up on the spelling game. How do you spell…Robbie? 'Robbie, wobbie, knicker knobby, full fobbie, double obbie, that's how you spell Robbie'. Derek? 'Derek, werek, knicker knerek, full ferek, double erek'. She was also a stickler for grammatical correctness, very quick to pounce on a split infinitive and absolutely strict about 'different from'.

Eleanor on the beach at Dalmeny, NSW circa 1949

Dad and Mum went on their first holiday alone when I left for Sydney University—on a cruise to Fiji. Later, they travelled a lot—trips always preceded by a lot of clothes planning and making by Mum—including lots of cruises. That was Dad and water again, and also the ease, he said, of only having to unpack once.

In her later life, her energies went into helping Dad on the property he bought and a great deal into their four grandchildren. When she and Dad moved back to Sydney, she would preside over family dinners every Sunday night, carefully rotating the favourite pudding of each child and grandchild, so everyone had a turn. It reminds me too of the welcome home dinners that were always there for me when I came home from school—pretty nearly always steak, onions and mashed potato followed by chocolate rum tart, absolutely delicious!

She was proud of but perhaps felt a bit overshadowed by her intellectually high achieving family, driven as they all were by their formidable aunts (known at the ''98 Aunts', three of whom lived in the family home at 98 St George's Crescent, Drummoyne). But she was pleased when one of them, nearing the end of her life in the old people's home, lifted her head from the pillow and said to her 'You were always the beautiful one, Eleanor'.

And she was.

Chapter 9

Enid Marion Walmsley (Née Shorthouse)

Stephen Walmsley

Steve's sister, Faye, was two years behind me at CCEGGS and a boarder. Steve visited her frequently when he was studying at ANU. A year older than most of us and the owner of a car, he was popular with the schoolgirls. I met him on one of these occasions and we became good friends when I started university the following year. Steve was my first husband and father of my two children Claudia and Joshua. He was to become a well-known judge. Marion was always my much-loved mother-in-law.

Robbie Henderson

Enid Marion Shorthouse (known always as Marion), was born in Neutral Bay, Sydney, on 30 September 1918 and died in Canberra on 11 February 2011, aged 92. She grew up in Greenwich, in Sydney's lower north shore, and was educated at Greenwich Primary School and Chatswood Girls High School.

She came from a musical family. Both of her parents played the violin; they met while playing in an orchestra. Both sang in the choir of their local church. Marion had a fine soprano voice, and took singing lessons at the Sydney Conservatorium of Music. For most of her adult life, she was in great demand to sing at weddings and other functions. When later in her life she was a farmer's wife, she played a leading role in the musical life of the Yass district, singing in Gilbert and Sullivan and other musicals.

Her father was a fitter and turner. Her mother never worked outside the home. Her father was never without work through the Great Depression, but at times money was tight, and midway through the Depression, a bank foreclosed on the mortgage on their home of ten years, the only house they ever owned.

She and my father, Lewis, married on 14 April 1945 and I was born on 5 February 1946. My late sister, Faye, was born on 7 October 1949 and my brother Mark on 1 July 1958.

Typically for a girl of her generation, Marion lived with her parents until her marriage. She worked from the time she left school at age 15, until her marriage just before the war ended. As it turned out, to a significant degree, her war experiences were affected by my father and his family.

Marion Shorthouse circa 1940

When the war started, Marion was working for Woolworths in the city as a typist. Several years later, she decided to take up nursing. By that time the war had been going for two years, and she thought this would be a good way to do her bit. She sat for and passed the NSW Nurses Entrance Examination, then regarded as an equivalent of the Intermediate Certificate, forerunner of the School Certificate.

For six months, she worked at Royal North Shore Hospital as a student nurse. But she was unhappy. She was probably too old to start nursing at age 23 after working in an office, with a certain amount of freedom. The fierce hierarchy of nursing did not suit her. She left nursing and applied for another clerical job. She was armed with the following reference:

To Whom It May Concern,
This is to certify that Miss M Shorthouse has been in the employ of this Company since June 1935 to the present date, 21st May 1941.
During this time she has been engaged as a typist and in general office duties at head office.
We always found Miss Shorthouse to be quick, accurate and willing, her work being carried out to our entire satisfaction.
Miss Shorthouse leaves our services of her own accord and we wish her every success in the future.
Woolworths Limited
Secretary

She was offered work by radio station 2CH. She was to stay in this job for four, very happy, years. The position was much more than clerical. The station had a policy of broadcasting music live by members of staff who were musically talented. She worked from offices at the base of the famous art deco building and tower.

2CH staff could take visitors to the tower's viewing platform, and Marion frequently took guests, including my father, to the platform. Marion became a member of the 2CH choir, some of whose concerts were broadcast on 2CH. Recitals from soloists, including Marion, were also broadcast. Staff members would be given gramophone records of their broadcasts[1].

Like many women of her generation, her life was a mixture of working during the week, (and Saturday mornings), leisure and looking for the right man to marry. She was 21 at the outbreak of war. She was good looking, vivacious,

[1] Marion bequeathed me several of those, one of which, fortunately, still plays.

gregarious and ambitious. She had a number of admirers and interests. She was a Girl Guide well into her twenties and an accomplished horse rider from her teen years until she was in her fifties.

Her war began with her twenty first birthday on 30 September 1939. She and her parents, her elder sister, Ruth, and other family and friends, gathered at her home for what was a dry celebration, since the family was chapel.

As was typical for 21sts of the time, Marion was presented with a ceremonial key to the door. This was a large, commercially produced key, in the shape of a 2 and a 1, made of wood, and signed by all who celebrated with her. At Christmas 1941, the local grocer (as he had always done) delivered a bottle of sweet sherry to her mother, who, (as she, the Baptist, had always done) poured it down the sink.

The early years of the war for Marion were happy. However, she was anxious, like most Australians, about England, and the added possibility of a Pacific war. Her father's people were from County Durham, in England's north, and she still had uncles and aunts living there. Their letters kept her in touch with how Hitler was affecting them.

Marion lived on the lower north shore throughout the war and throughout her life would recall her fear on the morning she heard that Japanese submarines had entered Sydney Harbour.

Marion met Lewis in 1943 at a YWCA dance in Sydney, an event designed to provide feminine company for the troops. He was at that time on leave from the Australian Imperial Force (AIF) in New Guinea. Thereafter they met rarely, until their marriage on 14 April 1945, and even after they married, they were apart for almost a year before his demobilisation on 3 January 1946. So that for most of their war years, their relationship was one of pen pals.

The two met at a time of tragedy for his family. In October 1943, Ted, one of Lewis' brothers, was killed by a Japanese sniper at Sattelburg Heights, near Lae in New Guinea. Ted was a member of the 2nd/17th Battalion, a Desert Rat, and had only recently escaped death in Alexandria when a German bomb dropped on his ship had failed to explode.

Many years later[2], Marion read a letter Ted had written to Lewis just before his death. His letter included the following:

---

[2] Lewis received the letter after his brother's death, and could not open it until decades later.

We have been in action against the Japs for a good while. Find him a tough nut in a lot of ways—more animal than human—and also cannibal but not much brains compared with the Germans. He is all right when you do just what he expects you to do, but do it an unexpected way and he is knocked right on his...

We have surprised him on almost impregnable positions and pushed him off easy—he would be so annoyed that he would counter attack time again, with little or no hope of success.

After it's over, we get quite a laugh out of things. When he is all set to go he blows a tone on a bugle or whistle and screams and makes all the noise possible, which of course is to our advantage as we know where he is coming from. It's all in though, no quarter is expected and certainly none given.

The Air Force has done a great job. We have seen some very decent bombings

[F]orty odd Liberators dropped over two hundred tons of bombs the other day and we had a grand stand view. They also fire thousands of rounds—with their half-inch cannon...

We see many types of planes... Libs, Fortress, Mitchells, Bostons, Hudsons and dive-bombers, not to mention the fighters—Kitties, Lightnings, Spitties, etc., so now, unlike the old Tobruk days, we have a decent top cover.

Nippon[3]*, of course, does his best, but is more or less shot out of the skies. We have seen several shot down, so now he usually comes over of a night; this morning early, we saw him dropping supplies to his troops (which I guess must be badly in need) about an hour after our planes came along and strafed the area where they had dropped.*

The country itself is very rugged—with high hills and deep gullies, hellish thick jungles and all open country is covered with kunai[4] *grass six feet or more high, as thick as it can grow, thousands of coconut palms, bananas, pawpaw etc., but very little of the fruit is ripe. We boil it as vegetable and it's not so bad, particularly the taro yam.*

---

[3] According to Wikipedia, both Nippon and Nihon literally mean 'the sun's origin', that is, where the sun originates, and are often translated as the Land of the Rising Sun.

[4] Wikipedia: Imperata cylindrica (commonly known as cogon grass /koʊˈgoʊn/, kunai grass /ˈkuːnaɪ/, blady grass, alang-alang, coon wool grass, kura-kura) is a species of grass in the family Poaceae. Red cultivars of the species grown as ornamental plants are known as Japanese bloodgrass.

We have not been living too bad. The dried vegetables are a wonderful thing—potatoes, onions, carrots, tomatoes etc., but would give a lot for a loaf of bread.
Well, old brudder, I think I have written enough and for this time, hope the address still finds you. Am looking forward to the time when, with elbow on the bar, you'll say 'Have another'.

Yours as ever,
Ted

In his early letters to Marion, Lewis described how he had been close to Ted notwithstanding that they were eight years apart. Lewis was one of eight. The family lived on the land, a property near Yass called 'Milford'. After his sister and other brothers had married or left home, he and Ted had worked together for years before joining up. As he later put it to Marion:

Ted and I were left together... Ted and I settled down and worked very hard. We ploughed new ground, sowed more lucerne and artificial grasses, built a modern shearing shed and improved the place such a lot. Ted was perhaps a little hard at times but admired by so many for his work and determination to get on in life. For four years, we were together every day and Marion its marvellous how attached you become when you are so much with a person. Ted travelled over most of Australia and New Zealand. I didn't travel quite so much but nevertheless went places. When separated, we used to look forward to seeing each other again, and the talks we would have about the good times and places we had visited!
Easter 1940 saw [sister] Nora married, we had a big party, lots of visitors and didn't we have a grouse time. It was the last that we were to have together. Of those present, Ted and another boy have been killed, and another boy a POW in Japan.
In the weeks that followed, the war [it] became more of a worry to us all. It was the 18 June, the morning after France surrendered, that Ted and I talked things over. Ted decided to enlist and agreed that I should stay behind and manage the property as well as possible.

I shall never forget that cold frosty night that I drove Ted to Yass Junction. It was mighty hard to say goodbye, being so attached to one another. Then such a gloom came over Milford.

Marion often felt from the time she met Lewis that she lived with Ted's ghost. He was so frequently on the mind of her husband to be, and later, at Milford, where there were many reminders of him, he was a constant presence and Lewis often mentioned him in his letters from New Guinea.

Marion was a prolific correspondent. She and her future husband began their pen pal correspondence when he was recuperating from malaria at a nursing home in Bowral. Sometimes, she would travel by train to see him there. In March 1944, he was sent back to his unit in New Guinea. He left by ship. One of his early despatches included the ship's dinner menu. At the time she received that menu, Marion received a coconut in the mail, with her name and address, and a postage stamp, all on the outside shell.

Then she received the first of what proved to be many letters, from New Guinea[5].

29 April 1944
My dear Marion,

I am in New Guinea and beginning to see just what it is like to be in forward areas…

It would amuse you to see the native boys, with their crop of fuzzy wuzzy hair and such lovely white teeth. They wear all different kinds of dress, really only pieces of old clothing that they pick up or may have had given them…

The coconuts grow in abundance, and a marvellous scene they create. From where I sleep, I've watched the sun rise—truly a magnificent sight in the tropics.

Yesterday, I visited my brother's grave, not where he fell, but in a new cemetery where he was reburied on 15 March. Just a little mound of earth, a simple white cross. As I stood there, it was oh so hard to realise that beneath that mound of earth lay all that remains of my own dear brother…

Responding, Marion mentioned she was now having piano lessons, and was to sing at church the next Sunday. The church was a recurring theme in her life.

[5] Although I have Lewis' original letters, I do not have Marion's.

She was a devout Christian. Lewis was not a believer, but he was brought up in the Methodist church, and the church was also part of his life, as the following suggests:

8 May 1944

> *Yesterday there was a special service, firstly a negro padre preached the sermon. He was a splendid speaker and his sermon was far more useful than lots we have had from white padres. He was assisted by a negro quartet and could those boys sing! You know, they swing their hymns and they reminded me somewhat of the Comedian Harmonists*[6] *whom I suppose you remember toured Australia just before the outbreak of war. The negro choir have made recordings but it was quite a treat to hear them in person.*

Lewis' work in New Guinea was repairing trucks, but often he had little work to do, and he developed an interest in making jewellery. But he needed some hard-to-get items. Marion became his main supplier. She would often be at Woolworths or Coles to buy a tube of Tarzans Grip, or sheets of emery paper. She would also have to scout for film, as film was in short supply in New Guinea.

In her letters accompanying these supplies, Marion would describe her life in Sydney. Fortunately, she and her father and sister all had safe jobs, so the family was financially secure. Her letters were positive. His replies would keep her up to date with New Guinea morale. Here is what he said after D Day:

2 June 1944

> *'Quite a cheerful expression on the faces of my mates and myself tonight when we received the news that the Second front has been opened. As yet, we have practically no details but I'm sure that this is 'the beginning of the end'.*

Sometimes he would describe the capture and use of Japanese equipment.

[6] A German all male harmony group popular in the 1920s and 30s.

(Late June) 1944

'Togo[7] in his hurry to get back to the fatherland left quite a lot of equipment here. Tools and trucks, which we are putting to use. The trucks are similar to American makes, and to my surprise are fairly well made. The lads are souvenir hunting, and have been rather successful. This writing paper is some of Togo's'.

By now, Marion (and many of her compatriots) had become adept at cooking and packaging cakes to be sent to New Guinea by airmail. She would send one off and then wait to hear if it had arrived in an edible state. Many did not. Some were lost or stolen en route. Others were attacked by mould.

She would be relieved when told a cake had arrived safely. A report of one safe delivery also updated her on other things:

30 June 1944

[Reports on safe arrival of the cake.]

'[My parents] pine for their loss' [i.e. of his brother]...

[W]e are told of great unrest in Germany and that Churchill thinks that the war will be over much sooner than lots of people think. Let's sincerely hope so.

[Thanks her for emery paper; tells her Brasso sent by his sister has arrived; says he will soon finish her brooch and will then make a locket.]

Having met her future husband, Marion slowly became accustomed to the idea of being a farmer's wife once the war was over. Lewis often reminded of her future role as unpaid kitchen help.

(Late July) 1944

[Suggests when writing to his sister, she says she would like to visit 'Milford' in October.] "You see in October, the folk at Milford will be busy with the shearing...so probably Mum and Nora [his sister] will appreciate your company very much."

---

[7] A reference to General Togo, used generically to describe the Japanese Prime Minister during much of World War 2.

Marion did write to her future sister-in-law, and she did go to Milford for the shearing and she did help out. Thus began a period of almost thirty years when Marion would help with the shearing every year, cooking for shearers, classers and roustabouts.

At this time, the two were not yet engaged, but Marion had begun to plan her trousseau, and in late 1944, Lewis promised to send 25 pounds to help with it.

She was delighted with the news, and even more so when the money arrived. Her sister, Ruth, whose future husband was also in New Guinea, was also planning marriage. The sisters planned their trousseaux together.

As appears in the next letter, writing to a member of the forces had its problems when there was any reference to classified information. All incoming and outgoing mail was read by censors. At times, parts of letters were blacked out.

31 July 1944

"Listen Dear,

I feel I must point out to you the fact that you wrote some military information in one of your letters. Actually unimportant, and I suppose you wrote it without thinking but it's wise not to mention such matters at all. The item I'm referring to concerns your friend Betty's husband..."

On 14 August 1944, Marion received a reminder to send safety pins and Tarzans Grip. So, their correspondence was back on safe ground. Shortly after, she received another coconut in the mail.

Late that year, the engagement was announced, and the two began planning their wedding. Lewis continued to keep her in touch with the New Guinea mood:

(Late September) 1944

"We listen in to the news about twice a day now and there's great speculation among the lads as to the day the European war will end."

Marion's family announced her engagement in December 1944 with a notice in the Sydney Morning Herald. She began to plan for her wedding. She and Ruth even discussed a double wedding. On 11 February 1945, Marion received a list of the people Lewis wanted invited to their wedding. The list included his siblings and half siblings.

Marion was a devoted monarchist, and in one letter asked Lewis if he knew of the impending visit of the Duke and Duchess of Gloucester. It would seem he did not share her monarchist views.

7 February 1945

Yes, I heard of the arrival of the Duke and Duchess, and also the speech the Duke made. I suppose a great deal of fuss will be made of them, wartime and all, and a great deal of public money wasted in entertaining them.

Many of Marion's letters to Lewis had reports of movies she had seen. His replies often contained descriptions of movies he had seen. The following, from New Guinea, was typical.

1 March 1945

I went to see the… 'The Rats of Tobruk' last night. I might say that I was not only greatly disappointed but disgusted to see such a poor effort, in fact it was an insult to the men who fought and died during the siege of Tobruk. They even brought a bit of New Guinea fighting into it. The jungle scenes in my opinion were taken in Centennial Park.

Marion's wedding remained at the forefront of their attention, but in March 1945, she was shaken by the death of her cat, Gloucester. When she reported his death to Lewis, he again reminisced about his deceased brother:

12 March 1945

Glad to hear that your frock is coming along nicely, because it will be finished in plenty of time now.

[Consoled her on Gloucester's loss]. I often became very fond of various dogs which I owned, and particularly so of a fox terrier which belonged to Ted. He got him as a pup in 1929 and he lived until he was killed by another dog in 1941. He was almost human, he would ride behind Ted on horseback, on the plough, pick the best seat in the car, in fact he would follow Ted wherever he went. Ted was away in the Middle East when 'Bob' was killed and I dreaded having to write and tell him the sad news. Mum often mentions poor old Bob in her letters, as well as Bluey, Ted's old chestnut horse. Now all three are gone.

Marion was married on 14 April 1945. By that time, her family had moved to rented accommodation in Chatswood. She gave up her work shortly before her marriage. The Yass Tribune Courier published the following description:

19 April 1945
A Chatswood Bride
Walmsley-Shorthouse

A very lovely ceremony took place on Saturday, 14th April, at St Andrews Presbyterian Church, Chatswood, which had been beautifully decorated for the occasion by friends of the bride, when Rev A. J. Parker officiated at the wedding of Marion, younger daughter of Mr and Mrs A. Shorthouse, of Chatswood, and Lewis (Craftsman, A.M.E.) youngest son of Mr and Mrs N. Walmsley, of Yass.

The bride, who was given away by her father, wore a charming old world frock of white French moire taffeta, with a tiered tulle veil held in place by a coronet of orange blossom, and carried a shower bouquet of white carnations and Cecil Brunner roses. She was attended by her sister, Ruth, wearing a period frock of pale blue embroidered French silk net over taffeta, with a shoulder length tulle veil, and carrying a bouquet of pink carnations. Mr Glen Walmsley attended his brother as best man.

During the signing of the register, Miss Peggy Garland sang Strauss' 'Devotion'.

During the reception, which was held in St Andrews Hall, the guests were received by the bride's parents, Mrs Shorthouse in saxe blue romaine with hat in tone, and posy of 'Sunburst' roses.

The bride chose powder blue crepe with matching hat for travelling, to which she added navy accessories, and a fur cape, the gift of her husband. After a short holiday at a seaside resort, the couple will spend the remainder of the bridegroom's leave at their station home, 'Milford', at Yass.

Marion continued to sing at others' weddings. At her sister's wedding, held shortly after hers, she sang The Lord's Prayer. Most of her recitals had a religious flavour.

Following her brief South Coast honeymoon, and visiting Milford, Marion went to live with her parents, as Lewis had to return to New Guinea. Soon, she realised she was pregnant. When Marion became noticeably pregnant, she decided to stop going to church, and informed Lewis accordingly.

It will be recalled that on 6 August 1945, the Americans bombed Hiroshima and on 9 August, Nagasaki. These events were reflected in correspondence Marion received soon after.

12 August 1944

Ever since Friday evening at seven o'clock, I've hardly left the wireless... It's been wonderful news to us all and I'm sure you folk back home will be happy also. Although at this hour, the war isn't exactly over; I will be very surprised if it lasts many days.

I had no idea that you will have to leave off going to church so soon. I thought it wouldn't show much for another six weeks.

14 August 1945

Everybody has been waiting patiently for the long expected news of the war's end... It seems a pity in a way that its being drawn out as every day means more deaths and suffering generally... Let's hope the end will come this week.

The next day, Marion wrote, describing events in Sydney after the bombing in Japan, including celebrations she had witnessed in the city. Meanwhile in New Guinea, the local people apparently bore the brunt of celebrations there:

18 August 1945

I suppose by now everything has quietened down after the celebrations. I guess the people went mad up around Kings Cross. It was pretty tame here...but a few of the native huts were burnt down.

21 August 1945

I was very happy this afternoon to receive your letter...written on the '15th'. Yes, it certainly is great news and I must say a real surprise for me as I kind of expected it to continue for at least another year as the Japs held such a tremendous lot of land on which there hadn't been a shot fired. [But] each day brings news of further surrendering.

Though the Pacific war ended in August 1945, the troops stayed in New Guinea, and wives and girlfriends in Australia were made to wait.

Late in 1945, Marion's father-in-law, who lived in Yass, became very ill, and Lewis applied for early release, to see his father before he died. He wrote to Marion:

January 1946

Usually, the Army takes its time. My claim went in on Monday and here it is Saturday night, and I'm just as much in the dark as ever. All I can do in the meantime is keep hoping that all will be well and that Dad will be spared, at least until I get home.

If my leave does come through though, and I reach the mainland, I should have an excellent chance of getting my release, and as you say, can be [ready] to start our married life.

But the Army came good, and Lewis got a ride home by air, unlike his colleagues, who followed by ship.

Marion was fond of her father-in-law. His illness was bitter sweet. It gave her husband his final ticket of leave, so she could become the farmer's wife she had long anticipated. But her father-in-law died on 16 February 1946, just days after her husband had got his final leave, a mere eleven days after my birth.

In February 1946, Marion and Lewis began their farming life together on Milford. It was to be their home and their living for most of the next thirty years. The farm ran Merinos, some beef cattle, and a few dairy cows.

Marion took happily to country life. She acquired her own horse, sometimes helping with the mustering. She learned to use firearms, suffering horrific bruising from the kick of a 12 gauge on her first go of it, on another, using the same 12 gauge to shoot and kill a brown snake in the household garden. She became accustomed to hearing farmers talk about things she did not usually discuss, such as the quality of a new cow's teats, or injuries caused by a shearer to a ram's pizzle. She joined the Country Women's Association (CWA). She was active in the Country Party, and was involved in several preselection battles in her local electorate.

Mark, aged 3, Stephen (in Canberra Grammar track suit), aged 15, and Faye aged 11, at Milford, 1961.

Marion, Mark and Faye at Milford 1961.

Throughout the 1950s and 60s she worked hard in the home, cooking for shearers at shearing time, and for farm labourers at other times. She helped run the management side of farming, and at times had her own small herd of cattle, which she would trade through the local stockyards so she would have some financial independence. Her social life was busy, with family, friends, tennis, church and music, at its core.

Marion, Stephen and Mark at Milford 1962.

In the seventies, after years of poor seasons and low wool prices, she and Lewis sold Milford and moved to live in Canberra. Lewis continued farming on a smaller scale, and found manual jobs in Canberra. Marion, for the first time since leaving Sydney, had the freedom to go back to work in an office. For her this was bliss. She was no longer at the mercy of wool prices or the weather. Her income, though modest, was at least steady and reliable. She met and made new friends. She bought, managed and then sold a small business. She continued her interest in the church and in music. For the first time in her life, she acquired a passport, and she made a number of overseas trips.

Sadly, Marion and Lewis lost their daughter, Faye, in 1980. She was only thirty. She died suddenly, after years of illness. She was not married, and she left no family.

Altogether, Marion worked for over twenty years in Commonwealth public service jobs, ending her working life as a librarian in the Dickson library in Canberra.

Both Marion and Lewis had active retirements. Lewis died in 2002 at 84, and Marion in 2011, at 92.

As a mother, Marion was gentle, generous and assertive. She had a great sense of humour. She held the firm view that men were somewhat inept, and needed guidance from women to reach their potential. She taught me some important things in life, such as the rudiments of cooking, feeling comfortable at the stove, and how to sew on a button, and iron a shirt. She advised me how to place trousers under a mattress overnight, to restore the creases. She would help with homework. She taught me how to swim.

She could be maddeningly protective. I recall when about eight, setting off up the road from my grandmother's home with my cousins on our way to the Liberty Theatre in Yass for the Saturday matinee. She waved to us until we were out of sight, prompting an older cousin to say, "You'd think we were going for a month." (I did not report that back to her.)

Years later, when I was 18, I was late home to the farm after a night out. Fearing I had been in an accident on the 50 km drive to the farm, she rang and spoke to the father of a girl several girlfriends before the one I was with, to ask if he knew where I was. (He was nice about it, and they both saw the humour.) I had not always found it profitable to fill her in on current romantic attachments.

I greatly missed her when she died. Fortunately, she retained her keen sense of humour up to her last day. Fortunately too, for the good of her fellow nursing home residents, for whom she was their shop steward, she retained her assertiveness all her life. She died when Julia Gillard was Prime Minister, and though she admired and liked her, Marion remained a conservative voter all of her life.

Chapter 10

Peggy Hilda Wheeler (Née Bell)

Philip Wheeler

I first met Pip Wheeler aged 12 with my school friend, Jenny Tange, when he was on home leave from Geneva. He was intriguing with his red shirt and long black pants; not the usual garb for boys his age. We became good friends when the family returned to Canberra permanently in 1961. He was very outgoing and the source of many introductions between the students of CGS and CCEGGS. Many hours were spent at his home in Red Hill listening to records, of which he had a magnificent collection, and drinking coffee. Pip's mother Peg was very tolerant, even when we set her dining room table on fire whilst having fondue. She encouraged us to visit and chat. We were there so often she became our friend too. She was generous, kind and full of interesting stories. Pip and I progressed on to ANU, eventually working together in the NSW bureaucracy and later in the Solomon Islands.

Robbie Henderson

Peggy Hilda Wheeler was born 28 September 1914 in Double Bay, Sydney, to English parents Basil Percy Bell and Hilda Louise Bell (née Peacock) who had migrated to Sydney in 1912—partly, so the received family story goes, because Basil had married 'beneath him'—the Bells being of the professional classes, lawyers in Kingston-on-Thames in Surrey, while the Peacocks were 'in trade' in East Sheen, a suburb of London. It wasn't quite banishment but it gave a flavour to my mother's upbringing because Nan Bell (as we called her) never quite let Peggy forget the perceived slight she had suffered at the hands of the Bell family nor the impact of the enforced separation from her own family at the other end of the earth in Australia. She remained resolutely English to the end of her life…

Unfortunately for Basil, the youngest of 13 children, the money that had provided an education and profession for his older brothers—mostly in the law—had run out and so he became an accounts clerk and studied in the evenings to gain some qualifications. Mum's memories of her early childhood were of straitened circumstances in rented accommodation in Ocean Avenue, Double Bay, where her 'bedroom' for instance was a curtained off part of a larger room; certainly no luxury. She attended the Double Bay Public School and was clearly bright since she was selected to attend Fort Street Girls High School, a selective high school located at the foot of Observatory Hill in the Millers Point area.

Peg Wheeler circa 1958

It would appear that Basil's studies were successful and that his career was solid if not spectacularly successful—the early straitened circumstances were replaced by a reasonable degree of comfort but Hilda/Nan Bell, presumably because of the difficulties of the early years in Australia, adopted a distinctly parsimonious approach to household budgeting and expenditure which persisted throughout her life and drove her daughter to distraction. The family moved to Melbourne in 1928 when Peggy was 14, they built a house in Kew and Peggy attended school at the Methodist Ladies College in Kew.

But although she did well, being dux of her class at the Intermediate Certificate, her parents shared the common view of many of their generation that girls did not need education and that view, combined with her mother's parsimony, resulted in her formal education being cut short after the Intermediate and her entering the workforce at a relatively young age. The onset of the Depression no doubt reinforced the decision. The cutting short of her schooling in this way was something she always regretted and it shaped her attitudes in many ways, not least in deciding that her own daughters were going to be given every opportunity and every encouragement to matriculate and undertake higher education.

By her own account, her working life was not unpleasant—she worked as a clerk at the T & G Insurance firm and became part of a circle of female friends which lasted her whole life. At some stage early in the 1930s, she met Fred Wheeler, my father, at a tennis club where they both used to play at weekends, and they started a long courtship which, Mum used to say, only resulted in marriage because of the outbreak of war. In 1939, Fred was offered and accepted a job as Economic Assistant to the Prices Commissioner, Professor Douglas Copland, which required a move to Canberra.

Fred had a similar experience to Peg in terms of having his school career at Scotch College cut short in favour of joining the workforce—with the significant difference, however, that it was not intended to deter him from further study but rather, in view of the economic uncertainty of the late 1920s and 1930s, to give him the security of a job while being able to pursue his studies part-time. He attributed this move to the wisdom of his father, Albert Henry Wheeler, a senior executive with Standard Oil who, Dad alleged, correctly interpreted the economic conditions of the time and took decisive action to give his son the best chance of combining job security and the opportunity for further education.

Equality of opportunity for men and women was certainly not common at the time and Peg's experience of limited educational options was more or less the norm for girls of her background unless they had exceptional talent in a particular area and/or a strong determination to do something outside the norm. Peg accepted the decision made for her, and even some of the justification for it, but it always rankled with her when she spoke about it later.

Nonetheless, the 1930s passed reasonably pleasurably and productively with Fred studying hard at Melbourne University and working in the State Savings Bank of Victoria and Peg at the T&G. Both lived at home with their parents but, together with other friends from university and work, managed to spend weekends away at the beach or in the country—both sets of parents disapproved of what was regarded at the time as rather 'fast' behaviour but, as Peg's close friend and bridesmaid, Eileen Brooks, said to me years later, the young things all 'liked getting away from their families for a bit of a practice whenever they could'…

The intellectual climate of the 1930s was also stimulating, particularly in the circles in which Fred was involved at the University of Melbourne—John Maynard Keynes' publication in the UK of his General Theory of Employment, Interest and Money in 1936 had an immediate impact on the thinking of social, political and economic theorists around the world, including in Melbourne where academic thinkers of the calibre of Professors Douglas Copland and LF Giblin were at the forefront of debate about the polity and the role of government in shaping it—a matter of immediate practical concern in the face of the high rate of unemployment and social dislocation caused by the stock market crash of 1929 and the resulting Depression of the 1930s. There was a feeling that good social and economic policy could actually do something to ameliorate the immediate problems and to put in place settings that would improve conditions across the board in the future. Fred participated in the discourse of the time, along with friends and colleagues such as Dick Downing, and Peg reported that she attended many social events with Fred, listening to all the talk going on around her and enjoying meeting the bright and the brilliant but, as she also reported, always feeling the lack of her own educational attainment and overwhelmingly unconfident about offering any opinion of her own.

Canberra in the war years and the late 1940s was, if anything, even more exciting on many levels—intellectually, politically, socially, and, for Peg, with the fulfilment of having children and being properly in control of her environment for possibly the first time in her life. Her daughters, Pam and Elizabeth, were born in 1941 and 1944 and then, in 1947, I arrived as the third and last child. Fred's career prospered—he quickly moved into the Treasury and moved up through the ranks, being highly regarded by the wartime Treasurer, Ben Chifley and travelling overseas with him on several occasions during the war and afterwards, to the UK and the USA. The Curtin Government of the time was paying great attention to planning for what should happen after the war and Fred was one of the senior Treasury representatives on many of the groups involved in this mammoth exercise. One of the outputs of this effort was the White Paper on Full Employment published in 1945 which became the blueprint for much of governmental action during the so-called post-war reconstruction period.

Peg made many close and loyal friends during this period with other young wives and mothers who were in a similar position to herself, mainly supporting husbands in the public service who, like Fred, were involved in providing policy advice to a Government that was consciously developing an independent identity for Australia and seeking to reshape Australian society. Heady stuff. Everything seemed possible and there was a confidence in government and public service circles that, by dint of good research and thorough policy development and management, they could collectively make a difference—and put the misery of the Depression behind them forever.

It is, however, notable that there were very few women involved directly, most were restricted to a supporting role although there were, amongst Peg's friends, many highly intelligent, not to mention formidable, women; in more recent times, they would themselves have been at the forefront and active participants in social and political discourse and in determining the resultant policy settings. There were some outstanding examples of successful career women, Pauline Fanning and Helen Crisp, for example, amongst Peg's friends but they tended to have professional qualifications such as Pauline's library degree, whereas those with generalist BA or no post-secondary qualifications, mostly concentrated on the role of housewife and mother. The ban on permanency for married women in the public service reinforced this state of affairs. No doubt these intelligent women had well-formed opinions and had input into the thinking of their husbands and thereby indirectly into the policy process but, for the most part, they were not at the table[8].

On the domestic front, using the analogy of the social contract theory of political economy, Fred said he and Peg had a contract in relation to their marriage—in return for being able to concentrate on his career. Peg was in full charge of the household and the upbringing of the children—and, in many ways, this is how things worked—Fred was frequently absent on work assignments, overseas with government delegations to Bretton Woods for example—and Peg managed very well without him. It is not entirely clear that she had much choice in the terms of this contract but she certainly abided by it and thrived on it, at least in the 1940s and 1950s.

Peg's stories about these years were about how everyone had to make do and how they all joined together in Canberra to do just that—during the war, with rationing in force, all sorts of things were difficult to obtain, including certain types of food, so they all 'made do' and, according to her, they helped each other and collectively did quite well! There were stories of lots of parties involving the making of highly intoxicating moonshine drink—the laundry copper in the Wheeler house at 6 Durville Crescent, Griffith, was evidently used for that purpose frequently—and there were picnics at places out of town—Coppins Crossing, Kambah Pool, Casuarina Sands—and Sunday drives to the pub at Collector which was conveniently just more than 25 miles from Canberra and therefore able to serve liquor to bona fide travellers from the capital.

Nicholas Brown's book *A History of Canberra*[9] records Peg's involvement during the 1940s as secretary to a Griffith Parents Group lobbying for the 'more systematic provision of services for children, mothers and families'. The group had Arthur Tange as its president and Brown ascribes to it success in establishing a local nursery at Manuka in 1944, and a play centre in 1945—I assume the one I attended, in Stokes Street, Griffith, in the early 1950s. This gels with what Peg told me about the flavour of life in Canberra in those years—a strong sense of community and working together to address shared needs. One account of her during this time was given to me by Kathy West, daughter of Harold and

[8] In similar vein, a collection of the stories of the wives of diplomats published under the apt title Wife & Baggage to Follow (edited by Rachel Miller, published by Halstead Press, 2013) demonstrates how wives and partners played a role, largely unrecognised in early days and how they came increasingly to be recognised officially over the years, at least by the diplomatic service. It is very entertaining as well as illuminating!

[9] Cambridge University Press, 2014

Elizabeth White and my erstwhile babysitter, who said that her predominant memory of Peg in these early days was that she was very lively and almost always laughing—a picture that I treasure.

At the end of 1952, the Wheeler family packed up and moved to Geneva, Switzerland where we lived until the end of 1960. Fred, having missed out to (Sir) Roland Wilson on appointment to the job of Secretary to the Treasury, accepted the position of Assistant Director-General and Financial Comptroller (Treasurer) to the International Labour Organisation (ILO)—with his usual caution, he took well over 12 months to accept the offer whereas Peg said she made up her mind she wanted to go on the spot, and go we did!

Life in Geneva was pretty good and Peg revelled in it—she was welcomed by the families of Fred's new colleagues—Raghunath Rao, his French wife, Juliette, and their daughter Sita in particular—and by Pat and Helen Shaw, old friends from Canberra who were there as Australian Consul-General and head of the Australian delegation to the UN in Geneva. Helen Shaw introduced Peg to Madame Magg, Geneva's answer to haute couture, and there developed a warm relationship that lasted the whole eight years in Geneva and resulted in a large and beautiful wardrobe. She had a cook and a housemaid, a car of her own and a high degree of independence to travel and explore the continent of Europe—sometimes with children in tow, sometimes with Aunt Dora or Uncle Sackville from England. Mum and I would visit Uncle Sackville and his wife, Aunt Gladys, in Lugano every spring where they went to 'take the waters', and Aunt Dora carted Peg off on coach trips, including one to Vienna and Budapest just before the Hungarian uprising of 1956. We had holidays in Italy in summer, in the south of France as well, skiing holidays in the Swiss Alps and in Austria and Germany, again with the Shaw family when Pat was appointed Australian Ambassador to West Germany. Peg accompanied Fred on work trips when he went somewhere, she was interested in visiting such as Vienna and Rome.

But the central focus was still on homemaking and the children—Peg became very involved in the school we attended—the International School of Geneva or Ecolint—organising the annual school fete on more than one occasion. She would unfailingly cooperate when I would blithely put up my hand in class to volunteer her services to accompany a class excursion, to the mountains, to a beach along the lake or, on one memorable occasion, to descend the side of the Salève, a large mountain just over the border into France which was 'climbed' in a téléphérique and from the top of which extremely steep paths led down to the bottom—Mum and the other adults, including the teachers, were almost unable to walk for days afterwards. But she never said no—with the result that I continued, with supreme confidence, to volunteer her services year after year.

This was perhaps the most fulfilling time of Peg's life—she was busy, active and, to a large degree, independent. Fred continued to devote himself to his career and that involved quite frequent travel to meetings away from Geneva, in particular to New York where the Governing Body of the ILO would hold meetings in the UN headquarters. This travel frequently clashed with school holiday times and so Peg would organise family holidays without him—and manage everything on her own with little fuss or bother. Fred was not a tourist by nature nor much of a holiday person—Peg was a natural at both, so it was no hardship for her to pack up the children and the dog and to set off on an adventure.

The house was always full of people—friends, Australian visitors, waifs and strays, classmates of my sisters who would come to our place after school and sit and talk in an adult and sophisticated manner for hours on end—or so it seemed to me, as I tried to eavesdrop! Mum would keep me out of the way as far as possible because she knew that, given half a chance, I would have joined in, to the mortal embarrassment of my sisters! We regularly had long-stay guests: children of Australian friends such as Judith White, Janet Crawford and Margaret Fanning; a young Czech woman called Eva in need of a place to stay was with us for over six months; and Gay Lindsay, a half-Australian whose parents flew in and out of Geneva in a rather mysterious manner (the father was reputed to be a gun runner involved in the Middle East), lived with us for over a year and attended school with my sisters.

Although Fred and Peg were not part of official Australian government circles in Geneva, they knew all of the Consuls-General and indeed were friends with them from Canberra days—after Pat and Helen Shaw left, there came Ralph and Dorothy Harry; Gordon and Gwen Jockel; and Laurie and Bonnie Arnott (the Arnotts additionally having taken over the Wheeler house at 6 Durville Crescent after our departure for Geneva). Fred and Peg regularly put on parties for visiting Australian delegations including one famous time when Harold and Zara Holt attended a cocktail party at the Wheelers—Gérard, the long-time official chauffeur for the Australian Consul-General held court in the kitchen and magnanimously dispensed copious amounts of liquor to the other drivers with the result that when the Holts got into the back of their limousine, instead of exiting by the front gate in normal decorous fashion, they were unceremoniously driven around the corner of the house and into the back garden, only narrowly avoiding landing up in the wading pool—the Holts emerged from the car somewhat shaken but quickly recovered their dignity and were whisked off by someone else. The memory made Peg giggle ever after.

Conditions of service at the ILO were very generous, including full home leave for the family every two years. This involved one month on the ship from Italy back to Australia, one month in Australia and then a further one month on the ship back to Italy, so three months in all. Fred was unable (and I suspect disinclined) to take off so much time so it fell to Peg to oversee and enjoy the travel—Fred would join the family in Australia for his part of the leave and then fly back to Geneva while the rest of us lazed our way on board the Lloyd Triestino boats MV Australia, Oceania and Neptunia, calling in at all sorts of interesting places on the way and quite often meeting up with friends in the ports where the ships called in—Alex Hasluck in Perth was a regular and Judy McIntyre in Djakarta on one occasion—and there were new friends made on board, many of whom subsequently called in on us in Geneva. Enjoy it, she did—and so did the children.

The worst part of home leave was that it always had to happen over the long school vacation in the northern hemisphere which meant staying in Melbourne in the middle of winter in houses that were positively spartan (i.e., completely unheated)—Peg and Fred would stay in the comparative comfort of the Windsor Hotel while we children were farmed out to one or other set of grandparents in Kew and Camberwell. Canberra was marginally better since by then most people were beginning to install central heating in their houses; Sydney at the end of home leave, where we used to stay at the Hotel Belvedere in Rushcutters Bay, was best of all in terms of climate and warmth!

In the late 1950s, the decision was made to return to Australia—Pam had already returned to study medicine at the University of Sydney in 1959 and Fred felt strongly that he did not want to be an expatriate for the rest of his career; nor did he want his children to lose their sense of nationality—something that was observable amongst the large international community in Geneva with the children, in particular, neither belonging to their country of nationality nor to the country of their residence, Switzerland. He was offered the prospect of more than one job to return to in the public service in Canberra and settled in the end on the role of Chairman of the Public Service Board. Peg would, I believe, have happily stayed in Geneva for many more years but was persuaded to support the move back to Canberra and, as always, made the best of it. She sent her beloved dog Bibo to the UK for six month's quarantine so that he could join us in Canberra shortly after arrival, and began the logistical task of moving the rest of us back to Australia.

Peg, Elizabeth and I spent a final month in London at the end of 1960 before sailing on the maiden voyage of the Oriana from Southampton, particularly important to Peg because of all the Bell family relations that she had re-established and developed during the eight years in Geneva. On arrival in Sydney at dawn on New Year's Eve, Fred came out on the pilot's boat to meet us and we sailed in through the Heads up the Harbour to Circular Quay. The Jaguar was unloaded from the ship and, with the colourful Swiss licence plates still attached, we drove to Canberra on 1st January 1961 to start/resume life in Australia.

Canberra had grown and changed considerably in the time we were away and, not surprisingly, lots had happened to friends and colleagues in the meantime. Peg found it different and not always easy to settle back—what she had been used to in the early Canberra days in terms of being able to drop in on friends unannounced and to share lives was no longer the norm; people were more formal, more hierarchical and, occasionally, quite stuffy. Peg found that difficult and it reinforced her natural shyness and reticence. There was of course a lot to do, finding and buying the house at 9 Charlotte Street, Red Hill, settling into it and starting a garden—not a strength of either Fred's or Peg's but, luckily, Peg was adopted by an Italian called Pasquale who announced he would come and set it up for her which he did by dint of planting everything in an absolutely straight line, not a curve or bend in sight—Pasquale and his son and extended family looked after the garden for the next 20+ years and ensured it never deviated from the straight up and down!

With my sisters away at the University of Sydney and subsequently marrying in quick succession in 1963 and 1964, Peg's role as head of household was much smaller than it had been and there were not the opportunities for alternative diversions that there had been in Geneva. She undertook voluntary work with the YWCA and with the Koomarri Homes, tuckshop duty at Canberra Grammar where I was enrolled, but I have no doubt that it was a much less stimulating existence than she had experienced in the eight years in Europe. They no longer entertained or went out with friends in the way they had in Geneva, and while there were social duties as a result of Fred's position, these tended to be a long list of diplomatic functions—national day celebrations and the like rather than social occasions with friends. Fred's job was very busy and he would very often ring at the last minute to cancel attendance in favour of pressure of work. Peg, having arrayed herself in one of her Madame Magg outfits, would simply have to put it back in the wardrobe and wait for Fred to come home later. She prided herself on always having a meal ready and waiting for him no matter what time he finally left work and, as a result, she did not make arrangements to go out on her own with friends at night—a self-imposed constraint which I could never see the sense of but it was written into her contract, it seems.

In hindsight, this last period of Peg's life—she died in 1975, one week after the Whitlam dismissal—while not exactly sad, was not as fulfilling as the two previous decades had been. The role as manager of the household was much reduced and I think there was less joy and laughter overall. Having resisted for years, she finally joined the bridge set and soon became a fine bridge player. She travelled to New Zealand and to the USA to visit Pam and Liz and their children but she was almost diffident in her approach to them, no longer the confident primary carer but rather grateful to be allowed to fit in for a time, so long as she wasn't too much bother…

But when she died at the relatively early age of 61, I was not so much surprised as pleased to hear from so many people about just how much her friendship had meant to them—in her own unconfident way, she had inspired loyalty and had shared many moments of laughter and pleasure with a wide range of people. This included many of my own friends—she was always interested in the thoughts and doings of the younger generation and one of her great pleasures still was to cook a Sunday roast for me and my friends while I was at the ANU. After I left Canberra to study at Oxford in 1969, several of my friends continued to visit Charlotte Street to have the Sunday roast lunch with Peg and Fred in my absence.

In keeping with the theme of this series of contributions, Peg's life was very much a story of her times—of native ability not prized and nurtured because of the cultural prejudice against the education of women, but subsequently seizing and enjoying the weird opportunities offered by the wartime years in the hothouse atmosphere of Canberra; making the most of life in Geneva when her role was at its most extensive, and, finally, of a shrinking of the horizons when that role reduced and there was no profession or career or other firm foundation to fall back on. This is a not uncommon story for women of her generation; nor is the fact that one of Peg's main aims in life—and her enduring legacy—was that her children should not be denied the opportunities she had herself missed out on—in that regard, it is perhaps a universal story about the aspirations of one generation for the betterment of the next. I still thank her for it.

Chapter 11

Anne Enid Frances Stewart (Née Purcell)

Pam Gray

Pam and I met in senior school at CCEGGS. When she first moved to Canberra, she lived close to my house and we rode to school together. She was very smart but was one of those people who always thought she had done badly in exams which she had not of course. As Pam was one of the Physics students, Pam's mother, Nan, drove us around and we were lucky to get to know her quite well. She was great fun and very kind hearted, much like her daughter. She enjoyed our stories as we did hers.

Robbie Henderson

Anne was rarely called Anne. She was Annie or Nancy when she was young and Nan when she was older. Born on the 5 June 1921 in Victoria, Nan came from a privileged and giving family but, as did women of her time in Australia, grew up under the shadow of two World Wars. Her father and her favourite aunt served in the First World War and her husband in the Second. Each of them experienced the horrors of war but came back with determined resolve to put war behind them and embrace the joys of peace and family.

As a result, Nan was largely protected from war and said of the Second World War, "It was a long way away." She readily acknowledged, "I lived a charmed life in the bosom of my family." And, in accepting this gift, she passed it on by becoming 'the bosom' of her own family. She was also a woman of substance who determinedly made her own life choices, as did all the women in her family—each in her own different way.

To know Nan, you need to know her family.

Anne (Nan) Stewart as a young woman

Mother: Olive (Née Smith, Previous Marriage Cook)

Nan was the elder of two daughters (Annie or Nancy and 'Sister Pam', as my mother called her). Their mother was Olive (Olive Maud), the middle child of three daughters. They were Ivy, Olive and Myrtle. In those days, plant names were popular for girls.

Olive was a caring mother and grandmother whose life revolved around her family, as did Nan's a generation later. She was a talented artist. I remember enormous oil paintings, one of irises (the flowers of the day) and another of a full-bodied snarling tiger coming at you out of the canvas. These images capture Olive. Like an iris, she was someone 'to be admired' yet she could be a bit of a tiger. Olive also embroidered and did crochet work beautifully.

In Olive's day, painting and needlework were what refined ladies did along with being hostesses. From what I could see as a child that meant having other ladies over to play cards with tea, cakes and dainty sandwiches served on fine china.

A sherry in a crystal glass would be offered later in the day. What is more, Olive did not only play cards, she played competitive Bridge. And, for sport, she played the refined game of croquet, but again she did not just play, she was a state level champion and apparently a fierce competitor.

Nan's mother, Olive

Nan too was 'a lady' who liked playing cards (Solo and Bridge), having tea parties and enjoying a sherry. She too played croquet (as a young woman and later in life) and was cultured (more literary than artistic). And, Nan too made a career of being a homemaker.

Nan was warm and funny with a good sense of humour (that at times could be unladylike) while Olive was warm and more straight-laced. And, although Nan was not as fierce as Olive, in her own way she too could be a tigress. She had a strength you could rely on. If there was some kind of injustice, especially to her family, she could be formidable. I remember, for example, when I was young, maybe 8 years old, and going to the Methodist Ladies College in Elsternwick (Melbourne), there was an incident and Nan went up to the school and challenged the Head Mistress with aplomb on my behalf.

When I say Nan was a 'homemaker', I didn't see her overdoing the housework. That just seemed to happen in the flow of things. What I did see was her relaxing in a lounge chair enjoying a cigarette with a book in her hand. Smoking was a mark of women's liberation in the war years. And, there were always books in our house. Nan was an avid reader of both fiction and non-fiction, a love of books that came from her father, Clive whom she adored.

Clive (William Clive) Purcell

Clive was from a close-knit family. In World War 1, he was an Anzac describing Gallipoli as "a terrible place". He then served on the Western Front 'mud and blood' and in other campaigns in France, commenting in 1918, "The Yankee boys are over here in large numbers and we Australians get along splendidly with them." The quotes are from letters he wrote to his mother and family. It is clear from those letters (now in the War Memorial collection) that he was a literary man (enlisted as a journalist) and, although brave and prepared to do his duty for God and country, a reluctant soldier.

Jim, Annie and Clive Purcell, 1915

Clive was the second of six children born to William (died in 1914) and Emina Purcell. His sister, Annie, was the eldest who served during 'the Great War' in the Australian Army Nursing Service (AANS). She was dear to Clive and later became Nan's favourite aunt. Then came Eaton who owned a property in Queensland.

He tragically died and, shortly after, so did his wife leaving behind two young daughters. Clive's younger brother Jim (Osmond James) was killed in action at Gallipoli 'one of the bravest and kindest soldiers who ever donned a tunic'. Clive missed him deeply. Then there was Mary Flora (no information). The youngest in the family was Sarah who never married but when her brother Eaton died brought up her orphaned nieces.

Of Sarah, Nan said, "She was a little simple but unexpectedly rose to the occasion and, of her own volition, took on those girls." Women in this family all had that ability 'to rise to the occasion'.

Clive's letters from the front, expressed in words (and between the lines) that he was disillusioned with war and the human cost. For example, after three months in Gallipoli (close to Christmas), "I wonder if the nations will still be warring on the birthday of the Prince of Peace?"

What sustained Clive and gave him the strength to endure was his family keeping him connected with loved ones, friends and home through letters and thoughtful parcels of food, socks, cigarettes and other personal goodies.

After the War that was supposed to end all wars, Clive married Olive and became the man of peace he was meant to be. He was a 'gentle' man, a family man who loved his wife and cherished his daughters. When Nan was growing up, Clive worked as a journalist ('the inky way' being his life long career) with a number of Melbourne newspapers (including The Argus and The Age) and then 'The Colac Herald' (for many years as the Editor).

Nan lost her beloved father, Clive, when he died suddenly from a heart attack at age 58, a tragic loss for his family. At the time, Nan was a young mother still living close to her family in Colac. I was 18 months (apparently, Clive adored me) and my brother was yet to be born so we missed out on our grandfather. According to Clive's obituary in The Colac Herald), 'he was possessed of a charming personality which endeared him to all who had the pleasure of his company'. These words could also have been said about his daughter and our mother.

Nan always spoke fondly of both her parents although she said it was Olive who 'wore the pants'. Clive and Olive brought up their daughters in Colac (Western District of Victoria) and holidayed at Lorne. And, although they were Anglicans, sent Nan and her sister, Pam, to a Catholic School. They wanted their daughters to have a good education and the Catholic School in Colac was considered the best.

Nan liked school (particularly History and Art History) and the pageantry of the Catholic Church very much appealed to her. I gather from Nan that the nuns (The Sisters of Mercy) were good educators—some of them inspiring—but Nan always referred to them as the Merciless Sisters. From what she told me, they could be rigid and considered 'weakness' (whatever that was) a sin.

Clive Purcell just before he died

Nan's Favourite Auntie Annie Purcell

Clive's sister, Annie Auntie (who Nan called Auntie Nam when young), was Nan's favourite aunt and an influential person in her life. Auntie Anne enlisted in 1915 in the Australian Army Nursing Service and served in Egypt (including at the Palace Hospital in Heliopolis treating the wounded coming from Gallipoli), in England and, on troop ships. She went to War in support of 'our men'. Annie never married (though apparently 'there was someone'). She kept working after the War, first working in India and then returning to Australia becoming 'well-known in Victoria's baby health movement' and a matron (see ref. Janet Scarfe).

Nan loved and looked up to her Auntie Anne who had a reputation for being a no-nonsense person. She was a strong presence in her family with a true and caring heart, the person the family turned to for help and advice.

Auntie Annie

Auntie Annie believed in women working—even women from privileged families who didn't need to work. She believed work was good for a woman—for her polish and character. So naturally, when my mother matriculated from school with good grades, her Auntie Annie insisted that she take up a career like nursing (seen by the family as 'a noble calling for a girl'), at least until she was married. Nan told her Aunt that she preferred 'playing ladies' to nursing. But, Auntie Annie was insistent and enrolled the unwilling Nancy in a Mother Craft

Nursing course in the city. Apparently, she lasted a few weeks and then quietly but with steely determination came home and never went back.

Nevertheless, Nan did work during the war years as a telephonist, a job that allowed her to live at home, 'play ladies' and also support the war effort (as women did in those days).

Sister Pam Todd (née Purcell)

My mother's younger sister, Pam (Pamela Ellen Emina), was another story. She was exceptionally clever and when she matriculated, she did not need to be cajoled into taking up a career. The problem here was the career she chose. She was determined to go to university and study science. Her parents, and even Auntie Annie, were not happy. Not only was science an unwomanly profession and one that may well deter potential husbands, the family all felt Pam would be wasting her time. After all, there was no promise of a career for a woman in science and it was deemed both unseemly and unwise to be too ambitious in a man's world.

The family reluctantly did let Pam go to university persuaded by her teachers (the nuns). Pam went on to graduate in science from The University of Melbourne with a PhD in biochemistry. While she was studying for her doctorate, Pam too supported the war effort back home in Colac working on farms.

Nan's Sister, Pam

Apart from post-doctoral studies in London, Pam never left Melbourne University and over the years became a highly acclaimed academic who did cutting edge research and was widely lauded for her achievements. Yet, at the same time, she was penalised throughout her career as a woman and had to take that in her stride. To avoid as she said 'that woman nonsense', she deliberately called herself Dr P Todd on research articles and sent her male postgraduate students (or other male members of her team) to deliver her international papers. She knew that in science a woman's work, however outstanding, was likely to be taken less seriously than a man's.

Pam did marry, someone she truly loved, David Todd. David was wealthy, urbane and not afraid of having a highly educated wife. But, when the time came, even he made her choose between her career and her husband. It really was not the one thing in those days for a man's wife to work as it reflected badly on the man and 'people would talk'.

Pam chose her career and, in doing so, lost the love of her life.

When she died, Pam left a Trust to The University of Melbourne for a scholarship in support of women studying science. She also left money to the Sisters of Mercy in Colac showing the deep gratitude she had for their support.

Nan and 'Sister Pam' were always close but so different. Pam didn't have children. Her life was science and her friends were either intellectuals or from the Bohemian art set in Melbourne.

Nan (neé Anne Purcell) and Allan Muir Stewart

In contrast, when you asked Nan what she saw as her purpose in life, she would say, without hesitation, 'to be a wife and a mother'.

Nan embraced being a woman of her time. Like the advertisements in the 40s and 50s of the young wife looking glamorous in a pretty apron welcoming home her husband after a hard day at work, that was Nan. And, she was naturally glamorous. Apart from lipstick and a little powder when she went out, Nan didn't wear makeup. Besides, I don't think she saw it was her duty to look glamorous for her husband. He was a man who would have loved her anyway.

And, Nan's household ran smoothly, seemingly without effort. She fitted in with her husband Allan's career in the Air Force and made his life her own. To Nan, being a 'kept woman' (her words) was a gift she was happy to accept. As the wife of an officer, she travelled (in Australia and overseas) in the days when many women didn't have that opportunity. There were Mess functions and much entertaining. Nan liked people and they liked her and she always had interesting and worldly people around her.

My brother, Tony, and I were very lucky to have Nan as our mum. We were loved and supported for who we were and what we did. Our dad too was a lovely man. As their children, we were doubly blessed.

My father (Allan Muir Stewart) and Nan met while he was home on leave from the War, then serving in the Pacific. Their wedding photo—like most photos of that time—showed the bride in white and the groom in uniform. My father was a Wing Commander in the Royal Australian Air Force (RAAF) and during World War 2 served in Australia, the United Kingdom and Papua New Guinea (Rabaul and Milne Bay). Like a lot of servicemen who spent time in Papua New Guinea, he came back with malaria. In fact, he had a bout of malaria shortly before he married Nan; the reason he appears thin and washed out in their wedding photo.

Nan and Alan on their wedding day (bridesmaid is Sister Pam)

After the War, Allan remained in the Services and we became a Services family. He rarely spoke about the War to us. Servicemen didn't in those days. They likely wanted to shield their families from the brutal reality of war and get on with enjoying a hard-won peace.

To my brother Tony's and my regret, we also didn't press my father for his war stories. We were too busy being self-absorbed baby boomers and enjoying the considerable fruits of the post war generation.

The very little my father did volunteer to us as we were growing up must have been important to him. He told us a number of times how he admired the bravery and humanity of the 'fuzzy wuzzy angels' who supported our troops in New Guinea.

And, he was haunted by the bombing of Dresden. He was there and was appalled, even from the air, by the firestorm that consumed that beautiful city and her people.

In the early 50s when I was young and Tony a baby, my father was posted to London for two years. And, while 'over there' in the 'home country', my parents took a tour of the Continent (as you did in those days) while my brother and I stayed in London (me with a friend's family and Tony with our nanny). On that tour, my father took Nan to Dresden where he was shocked again on the ground by the devastation. I think this was his way of showing Nan in vignette the terrible consequences of those nights of bombing, consequences Australians (apart from places like Darwin and Broome) had not experienced so personally or on home soil.

Throughout his life, my father always said to my brother and me, "Look after your mother." He loved Nan and her wellbeing was very important to him. But, he also treasured 'mothers'. He lost his own mother at a young age and knew how key a mother was to a family. He loved my mother for herself but also for how she made an art out of mothering.

Nan, Alan and children Pam and Tony in the early 1950s

If you asked my father what he wanted for his wife and family, he would have said for us to be well provided for and happy. While many men might express similar sentiments, for men (like my father) who went to war to protect their country, their way of life and their loved ones, such sentiments had a particularly strong resonance.

And, Nan was very good at being happy—and bless her heart, she had a way of making other people happy too.

Nan Was Her Own Person

My mother made our family and we all loved her for it and built our own lives, senses of 'self' and wellbeing on this strong foundation. She also led an active and fulfilling life of her own.

Once when I was a mother with two very young children and Nan was giving me advice on juggling children and my own needs, I said testily, "But, you had a nanny when we were that young." Smiling, she told me I had to understand she was in London (big time for colonials in those days) where there was lots to see and do in so little time that a nanny was necessary. I had to smile then too because my childhood memories were that she did not abandon us to our nanny, far from it. Nan was just way better than most at being her own person and being a mother. What's more, she often included us in her interests and what she was doing. Even though I was very young in London, I remember going to Trooping the Colours and seeing Princess Elizabeth in red on a horse. What's more, as Nan liked the theatre, she took me to the very best pantomimes.

Despite Nan following my father in his career, she had a mind of her own and her own opinions, many of them firmly held. However, even her most firmly held opinions were tempered with a 'live and let live' attitude to life.

For example, Nan was a staunch conservative. I don't think that ever really changed. Many of her contemporaries were also conservative with a strong respect for stability and establishment. But, she was well before her time on other issues such as gay rights. The daughter of one of her best friends announced she was gay. Nan, at first taken back, reasoned with the girl's mother that if they couldn't accept and support gayness, they would lose someone they loved and that was not going to happen. If we'd had the 2017 Same-Sex Marriage Survey in the early '60s, Nan may well have voted 'Yes'.

Nan was also supportive of the rights of women (like her sister) to have equality in male dominated occupations. Her only sticking point was women being priests or pastors. She was happy to go to their services, take communion and have them as friends. But, she preferred the status quo and believed men should be the true custodians of the Church.

Nan had many friends including two long-term friends Auntie Flora and Auntie Carol (not our real aunts). Our families were close, so close that their children were (and still are) like our brothers and sisters. Both these aunts were motherly and each was a reflection of Nan.

Auntie Flora Gillis had five children, a Bachelor of Arts and loved books. Nan and she were always reading and talking books and they shared a raunchy sense of humour. While the mums were talking, we children were let roam the streets of Melbourne like a gang of little street urchins. When we came back, there would be tea around a big table and lively discussion with all children included (whatever our age). At Auntie Flora's and Uncle Dick's, even doing the washing up was fun.

Auntie Carol (Haywood) was a warm motherly lady but also a 'party girl' who loved a good time and people. Uncle Tom flew with Cathay Pacific and they lived in Ceylon (now Sri Lanka), Sydney and Hong Kong. Whenever we visited the Haywoods, Auntie Carol and Nan would spend their time together talking, lunching and sightseeing, then they might end up in the evening with their husbands at the Cathay Pacific Club where they were invariably the centre of attention.

Auntie Carol and Nan would also think of us children and what we might like as treats. For their daughters (me and Auntie Carol's only child Susan), it might be taking us out so we could buy dresses, have high tea and 'play ladies'. They always made me feel good about being a girl.

My dad also admired Nan for her femininity telling us that she was good at using her feminine charms to get what she wanted. Apparently, in wartime, she would stand on a train platform with a suitcase looking petite and pretty and before my father had a chance to meet her, she'd be surrounded by guys in uniform all jostling to offer her their help.

More Friends in the Services and Canberra

With my father in the Air Force, we lived in many places, making a new home and life wherever the Air Force posted him. My parents were close to many Air Force families who were lifelong friends, a number who were also like second parents to us children. My brother and I were very lucky having so many adults looking out for us.

In the early '60s, all three Services moved to Canberra and the ACT became our most permanent home. In Canberra, Nan and Allan caught up with many Service families they had known for years as well as making new friends many of whom also turned into life-long friends (like quite a few of the neighbours in our street).

For the first time in Canberra, Nan was able to lead a more settled life (and Tony and I were getting older) so she decided to train as a secretary. After graduating, she won a job working as the secretary (more like office manager) to the Head of the Yarralumla Nursery (Parks and Gardens).

Parks and Gardens loved her. It was said that she ran the place. From the young apprentices and landscape gardeners, to post graduate students and high-level management, she looked after everyone, knew all their jobs, took a keen interest in Botany and, because of all this, could type up their correspondence, articles and theses without the need for direction.

Like women did in those days (and still do), Nan used her womanly skills (such as intelligence, warmth, wit and organisational ability) to the benefit of her workplace. She was likely underpaid for the calibre of the work she did (unfortunately often still true for many women today). This situation though didn't bother Nan as she (the 'kept woman') had the luxury of working for the love of the job rather than the money. In this, she felt liberated.

Later in Life

When my father died, Nan lost her 'rock' and life companion. But, being her own person, she rallied and became, if not 'a merry', a happy widow making a life for herself surrounded by family and friends. She also kept playing ladies and playing cards. Maybe in honour of her mother, Olive, she also took up competitive Bridge and croquet (played at the Croquet Club on the lawns of The Hotel Canberra where the ladies of yore would have chosen to play).

Sadly, in her late 70s, Nan started to lose her 'self' to dementia (and my brother and I started to lose our lovely mother). For a few years, we as a family were able to support her at home, but the time came when she ended up in a nursing home. My brother and I felt wretched and Nan felt abandoned.

There were times early on when the real Nan shone through. She used to smoke with fellow 'inmates' in the courtyard next to the grotto (a half-buried bathtub) sheltering a stature of The Virgin Mary. This was a Catholic facility that reminded Nan of her childhood with the nuns. Her inmate friends were a lively bunch and used to joke with us that it wasn't so bad being 'gaga' as you could enjoy the same conversation over and over. But, as happens in nursing homes, these 'friends' moved on in their dementia journey and Nan's dementia worsened. Visiting her was heart wrenching. When you came, she would light up but when you left, she would beg you to stay. And, she didn't remember how often we were there or how many visitors she had. Despite her failing mind, to the end, there were glimpses of the old Nan and bless her she never forgot our names.

Sadly, on 6 February 2007, we lost Nan.

Final Comments

In sum, Nan enjoyed a privileged middle-class life but also a simpler one by today's standards. The houses we lived in were modest. As I was growing up, we had one car, one fridge and, when there were TVs, one TV. As children, we did not have an abundance of toys. My family and the other families I knew were not as entitled as we seem to be today. They took what life offered and made the best of it.

Nan's legacy as a good wife and mother (and all the good men and women in her story) remind me that the strength of any society (whether in war or peacetime) is its people, its men and women and the mothers and fathers who nurture the next generation.

Nan chose to be a wife and mother. Her Aunt Annie and Sister Pam chose to be career women. The struggle many women face today is trying to do both.

References:

1. PURCELL: Annie Watkins Bennett Viz. Janet Scarfe (2015) East Melbourne Historical Society.
2. The Purcell Papers. PR84/096: Australian War Memorial.
3. Death of Mr Clive Purcell. Editor of 'The Colac Herald for Many Years'. Held in Very High Esteem. The Colac Herald, January 22, 1948.

Chapter 12

Katherine Elizabeth Saunders (Née Rolfe-Rogers)

Denis Saunders

Denis was one of the boys in my physics class. He also lived close to the CGS and not far from my house in Red Hill and that of his close friend, Geoff Furnell. Denis became very friendly with my friend, Helen Nicholls, who also lived close by and as a result, a lot of walking and bike riding took place up and down Quiros St. The Saunders had a coast house at North Rosedale and this became the venue for many enjoyable weekends with music and sun for all of us. Mrs Saunders (Mouse) and Wing Commander Saunders were great hosts and extraordinarily kind to Denis' friends. Denis and I studied science together at the ANU. He was good at it; his love of the subjects and his devotion to birds, the feathered kind, led to a very distinguished career in the CSIRO and environmental protection.

Robbie Henderson

Katherine Elizabeth Rolfe-Rogers was born at Hatton in Ceylon on 19 November 1920 to Ranville George Rolfe-Rogers and his second wife, Katherine Anne Devereux (neeé Moore). She was the eldest of their three children. When her mother first laid eyes on her, she said, "She is all brown and furry like a mouse." So while she was christened Katherine Elizabeth, Mouse she became, and very few people ever called her Katherine.

Mouse also had a half-sister, Helen Anwi, whose mother died of blood poisoning a month after giving birth to Anwi (as she was known throughout her life) in March 1917. Mouse's was a highly dysfunctional family. Anwi was adopted by her paternal grandmother, Annie Matilda Rolfe-Rogers soon after her birth.

Her father and stepmother had no say in her upbringing, schooling or any other matter. Mouse's parents were married on 29 May 1919 in Glasgow. Mouse wrote many years later: 'I have a wedding photograph of the happy pair and bridal party. I have never seen a more miserable group, not a smile anywhere'. There did not seem to be much affection between members of the family.

Mouse was a classic child of the British Empire. When she was born her father was a tea planter on Emelina Estate in the centre of Ceylon, and the family lived the life of the Raj. She accompanied her mother to Scotland when she was five. They stayed with her maternal grandparents for four months, which she hated. As she summed up the visit later, she stayed 'in a large, grey stone house, with grey weather, and grey people'! She wanted to know where the sun was and wondered if it ever did shine in that god-forsaken dump. They returned to Ceylon where her father then had a job as a surveyor building the railway line between Kandy and Trincomalee. When she was seven her family life changed dramatically. She and Anwi were taken to England by their grandmother, Annie Matilda Rolfe-Rogers, who looked after Mouse for most of her school years. Her grandmother had left her husband, Arnold Rolfe-Rogers, in Argentina after he had an affair with the family's nanny, who he subsequently married, and they remained in Argentina.

The life of the Raj! Mouse with her family and guests on the steps of their bungalow on Emelina Estate, Ceylon in the early 1920s. Back row: naval officer from HMS Hood, Kate Rolfe-Rogers (Mouse's mother), Annie Matilda Rolfe-Rogers (Grandmother) Naval officer from HMS Hood, Ranville George Rolfe-Rogers (Mouse's father). Front row: Admiral (the dog), Mouse, Anwi (Mouse's half-sister) and another dog (name unknown).

Mouse and Anwi were sent to Charters Towers, a boarding school at Bexhill-on-Sea, Sussex. This change from life in Ceylon to boarding school in England under the stern eye of her grandmother must have been hard for a little girl, who scarcely knew her parents, felt the cold badly after the tropics, suffered terribly from chilblains and had to put up with awful school food.

Both of her parents had served in the air force during the First World War. Her father initially served as a 2nd Lieutenant with the Royal Worcestershire Regiment in France in early 1915, broke his shoulder in the trenches, transferred as a pilot in the Royal Flying Corps in 1916 and became a foundation member of the Royal Air Force in 1918. Her mother was a member of the Women's Auxiliary Air Force (WAAF). They met at RAF Scampton towards the end of the war. When the Second World War broke out in September 1939, her parents reenlisted in the RAF and WAAF. At that time, Mouse was suffering from appendicitis and had to have her appendix removed. However, on 23 May 1940, when she was fit enough, she joined the WAAF as an airwoman. After two weeks of basic training at RAF West Drayton, she had three weeks of training as a plotter at RAF Leighton Buzzard, and was then posted as a plotter to Head Quarters 11 Group RAF Fighter Command, Uxbridge. The Hurricane and Spitfire squadrons of 11 Group were closest to the German Luftwaffe bases, and bore the brunt of the fighting during the Battle of Britain in the summer of 1940. It was from the plotting room at Uxbridge that the Group Commander, Air Vice Marshall Keith Park controlled his fighter aircraft, with the WAAF plotters, including Mouse, pushing symbols representing numbers and heights of enemy and friendly aircraft around a table, which represented a map of the south of England and the English Channel.

She was on duty one day in September 1940 during the height of the Battle of Britain, when the Prime Minister Winston Churchill lumbered down to the bunker, in which the plotting room was located, and asked the Group Commander about the state of his reserves. AVM Park replied to the effect that his fighters were either in the air, on the ground refuelling and rearming or had been destroyed; he had no reserves. Mouse served in a historic role at a critical time and was subject to horrific enemy air raids on many occasions at Uxbridge and London during the Blitz.

In May 1941, Mouse was commissioned in the WAAF as an Assistant Section Officer and spent a month training as a code and cypher operator at Oxford, learning encoding and decoding operational orders. After a brief posting to an Operational Training Unit at RAF Little Rissington in Gloucestershire in July 1941, she was posted to 15 Group RAF Coastal Command in Liverpool. She later wrote that it was a 'bloody awful place, but the work was interesting'.

Katherine Elizabeth (Mouse) Rolfe-Rogers in the early 1940s.

In January 1942, she sailed in a troop convoy to Alexandria, Egypt. On the same ship was Pilot Officer Allan Messer, a newly qualified Western Australian Royal Australian Air Force pilot, posted to the Middle East to serve with the British 8th Army. They fell in love and were soon engaged to be married. Mouse's WAAF superior officer was one of her mother's friends. On hearing that Mouse intended to marry Allan, her Section Officer took her aside and asked if 'this colonial comes from the right drawer'? Mouse's reply was to the effect that she did not care which drawer he came from, she was marrying him, and that was that. They were married in May 1942, and by all accounts were very happy. But just eight months later, on 29 January 1943, Allan was killed when his aircraft disappeared into the Mediterranean without a trace on a flight from Egypt to Nicosia, Cyprus. Mouse was devastated, and the depth of her loss was shown for the rest of her life, as she always had one photograph of Allan Messer in uniform with his pilot's wings prominently displayed in the lounge, and two smaller photographs on her dressing table in every house she lived in. After Allan's death, Fenella Boyle, her greatest friend and fellow WAAF officer wangled a transfer for Mouse and herself to Nairobi, Kenya. It was while in Kenya that Fenella wrote a poem *On Personality* which no one in Mouse's family knew existed until her children were sorting out her estate after her death in June 2009. It is worth printing here as it says a lot about Mouse at that time, and for the rest of her life.

I've come a long way now, a long way and seen many things:
here are love, and death, and courage, there are sorrow,
and the deep heart's grief yes, and there is despair,
creeping up, clutching sometimes from the underworld;
and there is laughter and the green grass
and the birds singing.
All these,
and also there is release and joy in flying,
in wandering in the high cloud country
the pure perilous upper air,
free and alone as God is free and alone;
also there are friends, good friends
(God keep us our friends).

and of all these things that I have seen and that I do not forget
I think the greatest of them all is courage
for to love greatly, there must be courage, such courage; also to die greatly,
and above all to live
to go on, to take these things
sorrow and love and death and delight
to take them and use them and build with them
(the ingredients, the raw stuff of life)
to build with them the fortress of life
the personality, the strong ship

for when the moment of destiny comes and the time for building is done
then the page of time flicks over, and there it is, uppermost,
the next leaf in the book
it is then that the soul is launched to sink or swim in that ship,
to go on with the great journey. O it is for that day
that the ship is built
that it is built of love, and grief, and delight,
and welded with courage.
I've seen so many brave people
especially in these last years
I have met with such gallantry, so much courage;
but isn't it strange,
isn't it curious
that of all the names, the person who has shown the greatest courage I have met
should be called of all things, Mouse?

Pilot Officer Allan Kenneth Burt Messer (RAAF) and Mouse in Cairo early in 1942 before they were married. Allan was killed on 29 January 1943, eight months after they were married.

Allan Messer, Mouse's first husband. This photograph was displayed in Mouse's bedroom from the time Allan died in 1943 until Mouse's death in 2009.

While on holidays at Molo in the Kenyan highlands, Mouse met Eric Saunders, an Australian Catalina flying boat pilot, who was attached to 209 RAF Coastal Command Squadron operating out of Mombasa, ranging over the Indian Ocean. Eric completed his operational flying tour in September 1943 and was posted to Army HQ East Africa. During that posting, in late November 1943, Eric flew Mouse in an obsolete twin-engined Avro Anson from Eastleigh in Kenya down the Nile River to Cairo; a flight of over 20 hours.

Unfortunately, apart from several lines in Eric's Flying Log Book, there is no stated reason for this flight together. They returned to Kenya in mid-December by BOAC's commercial flying boat service. They were married in the

Anglican Cathedral, Nairobi on 22 January 1944. In March 1944, Eric was posted back to the UK. They flew to Cairo by commercial flying boat but had to be off-loaded there as Eric had a bad attack of malaria. They then went to the UK, Mouse to Bedford, England, and Eric as an instructor at 131 Operational Training Unit at Killadeas, Loch Erne, Northern Ireland. Mouse resigned her commission in May 1944, as she was pregnant. As a result of her war service, she was awarded: the 1939–45 Star; the Africa Star; the Defence Medal; and the War Medal 1939–45. Rosemary Fenella, her first child was born in Bedford, England in August 1944.

Squadron Leader Eric Comber Saunders and Section Officer Katherine Elizabeth (Mouse) Messer at their wedding reception in Nairobi, Kenya 22 January 1944.

Mouse seldom spoke about her war experiences, except to comment on inaccuracies of documentaries about the period. The period 1940 to 1945 was tumultuous for her, with a period of great loss and sadness, and subsequent happiness. When she did comment on the period, she said she was personally grateful for the war, because it resulted in her meeting and marrying two good looking, young Royal Australian Air Force pilots, and moving to Australia as a result. While she may have been lucky, it says a lot about Mouse that not one, but two smart young men chose her. But for the war, she probably would have been a typist in an office in London and remained in UK for the rest of her life. In Mouse's case, war did change everything.

Eric returned to Australia in mid-1945, having been away for four and a half years. Mouse and Rosemary sailed into Fremantle in 1946 on one of the many 'bride ships'. There they met Allan Messer's family in Perth. Mouse remained close to them for the rest of her life. She and Rosemary then flew to Melbourne where they met the large Saunders clan; Eric being the youngest of six children. This was much more confronting, because Mouse was not quite what the family expected.

Eric had left Australia in late December 1940 aged 21, as an Airman (the lowest rank in the Air Force). He seldom wrote letters home in the time he was away, and returned as a Squadron Leader, with an English wife and daughter, neither of whom his family knew much about. In spite of remarking very early after her introduction to his family when served roast pumpkin, "In England, we only feed pumpkin to the pigs," over the long haul, Mouse won over most of them, was won over by most of the rest, and was ever polite to those not fitting into either camp. She had great affection and respect for both of her mothers-in-law, who were great supports to her. However, she was a stranger in a strange land, and in one letter to her mother, she expressed her feelings about the life she was living. Her relationship with her mother can be determined from the response from her mother, which was to the effect that; 'you have made your bed, you just have to lie in it'!

With Mouse and Rosemary re-united with Eric in Melbourne in 1946, the family started 21 years of post war Australian Air Force life. Their second child, Denis Allan was born in Melbourne in April 1947; he was named after Denis Saunders, one of Eric's brothers who was killed while serving with 10 Squadron RAAF in UK in May 1943, and Allan Messer, Mouse's first husband. Young Denis had become a living war memorial.

Service life consisted of various postings around Melbourne, then to RAAF bases at Rathmines in NSW (August 1948–June 1950), Momote on Manus Island (July 1950 to May 1953), and Pearce near Perth (June 1953 to April 1955). The family had 16 months in Melbourne, then Mouse accompanied Eric to Djakarta with the Australian Embassy in Indonesia where Eric was the Services Attaché (September 1956 to August 1958). Another posting to Melbourne followed, then in January 1961 came Eric's final Air Force posting, to Canberra. During this Air Force period, Mouse had her own careers within Eric's. She was a member of the network of Air Force officers' wives which offered support of each other. During the posting to Manus, she was the QANTAS agent. In 1954, Eric was made a Member of the Order of the British Empire; the post nominal was MBE. Eric referred to this as 'Mouse's Bloody Effort'; almost certainly in recognition of her support to his career. During their period in Indonesia, Mouse accompanied Eric on nearly all of his official travels over the archipelago, taking detailed notes on infrastructure such as roads, bridges, aerodromes, etc. These notes were passed to Australian intelligence. In Canberra, she worked with Jean Senger, a real estate agent. Mouse handled the rental side of the business.

Her nickname Mouse was not apt, as a less mouse-like woman would be hard to find. In early 1956, when she and Eric were making preparations to go to Djakarta, they had to obtain Australian diplomatic passports. Mouse happened to be in Eric's office at Victoria Barracks in Melbourne when he was rung by an officer from External Affairs. He informed Eric that he was arranging their passports but had struck a glitch. He noted Mouse was not a naturalised Australian, and there would be a problem issuing a passport to her. He asked if Mouse would arrange to take Australian citizenship. Eric held the phone aside to put the request to her. She responded, "You tell that son of a convict peasant that if he thinks that I will pay 10 shillings to become one of you, he has another think coming!"

The man on the phone said, "I understand the problem Wing Commander, I will see what I can do." Mouse was probably one of the few non-Australian citizens to have been issued with an Australian diplomatic passport.

In 1958, while still in Melbourne, the family had a holiday in Moruya on the south coast of NSW. One day during that holiday, the family found itself lost in North Rosedale. Mouse fell in love with the area and used part of her legacy from Allan's family estate to buy a block with a wonderful view of Rosedale beach and Jimmy's Island. "What a bloody silly thing to do," said Eric, "we'll never use the block." Not long after that, he was posted to Canberra, and the family then built a cottage on the block. Mouse funded it and provided a lot of the labour. Mouse and Eric spent as much time as they could at the cottage.

In 1967, Eric retired from the Air Force and moved into real estate in Batemans Bay. Eric conducted the sales and valuation side, and Mouse was the rental property manager. She was particularly good at this, but on rare instances followed the Basil Fawlty School of Business Management. On one occasion, someone rang on Boxing Day to make enquiries about renting a cottage the following Christmas. The rest of the family only heard one side of the conversation which went something like this. "Next Christmas?"

"Yes, we should be able to find you something suitable at this notice."

"Yes, people leave the cottages clean, but then we go in and mess them up so people like you can feel at home!"

Mouse was a loyal and devoted wife to both of her husbands. She wore both of her wedding rings, side by side, until the day she died. In fact, over the years, they became so thin she had them fused together so they would not break. Several photographs of Allan were always among those of Eric, her children and grandchildren on the walls and shelves of every one of her many homes. She saw herself as Eric's wife; she would have none of this modern partner thing. But their 59-year marriage was a true partnership, and rather more equal than Eric might have imagined. She never really adjusted to his death in August 2003, was very angry with him for leaving her alone and missed him desperately for the rest of her life.

As a mother, Mouse was not Mother Earth. Given the lack of affection she was subjected to as a girl, this was hardly surprising. However, she was mother lioness in defence of her cubs and grandcubs should anyone criticise or pose a threat to them. Mouse was left-handed, and in the early 1950s, she marched to Bullsbrook Junior School to straighten them out on the school's misguided attempts to make Rosemary, who is left-handed, write with her right hand. Despite the lack of overt affection, she loved her children and grandchildren dearly, was in constant contact with them and was extremely proud of them and their achievements; she was a tower of strength in their adversities and generous to a fault.

Mouse often protested that she, like Winnie the Pooh, was a bear of little brain, but she was widely read, had very good general knowledge and held strong views, particularly about politics and politicians, and was happy to air them. She was a very shrewd judge of character; she could smell a villain at 10 paces. She was always up to date, followed current affairs closely, read her newspapers from cover to cover except for sport. After Eric's death, she took on her own business affairs. She was very well-organised. When she bought into the stock market, she began to read the business section of her newspapers diligently, and sought information about any activities reported upon in relation to companies in which she held shares.

Mouse and Eric Saunders at Batehaven, NSW in the late 1990s.

She never regretted coming to Australia; she loved the country and studied its history closely. In 1972, she went back to UK with Eric for her only visit to the land she spent her formative years. She said that visit was sufficient for her, and she saw no reason to visit again. During that visit, she and Eric also went to Portugal to visit Fenella Boyle, her friend from Mouse's WAAF days. Although she and Fenella corresponded from the time Mouse left Kenya in 1944 until Fenella died sometime in the 1980s, that short visit was the only time they saw each other.

During a service life, constantly on the move, Mouse and Eric had no opportunity to buy a home. Their first was a small government house in Red Hill, Canberra in 1962 after nearly 20 years of marriage. Then after moving to the coast, they had six homes from North Rosedale to Batemans Bay. They designed and built four of these, and Mouse was the major influence in their design and décor. The design and décor reflected their life together, and the family experiences in the many places they lived.

With her service background, Mouse could call a spade a bloody shovel, but she loved the English language and used it beautifully. Her wry, dry observations were often right to the point. For example, when she decided to move into low residential care the year before she died, she dreaded the thought of going into the high care section. When she was moved to that section, she told her children on several occasions, "This is a most unsatisfactory."

Mouse was not someone who made her faith and religious beliefs obvious to others. But she had great faith that when she died, she would be joining Eric wherever he was. It was fairly clear that once she met up with Eric, she was going to give him a piece of her mind for leaving her nearly 6 years earlier. What was not clear was what she would say to Allan, her first great love, who to her was ever 23?

Acknowledgement

This chapter incorporates material from the eulogy that I gave at my mother's funeral. The eulogy was written with considerable input from my sister, Rosemary Crowther, and I greatly appreciate her contribution.

Chapter 13

Marjorie Jeanne Cooper (Née Lovett)

Diana Cooper

I met Di when we were 9 years old at CCEGGS and we became good friends. We spent a lot of time together on the monkey bars and collecting bugs and things that crawled. I loved visiting her house in Yarralumla as things were so ordered and English. My mother was a great reader of the English Women's Weekly and many of the things advertised in it; Marmite, Hovis and Lucozade were in the Cooper's house. Di also had special English shoes which I coveted. It was all so exotic. When the family moved to Red Hill and Di returned to CCEGGS, we had many parties at their house and saw Mrs Cooper frequently. She was always very sweet and welcoming and offered us tea.

Robbie Henderson

My mother, Marjorie Jeanne Cooper (née Lovett), was born on 4 January 1920, a date she found handy for remembering her age. "It is the same as the year," she would say, meaning the last digit. This worked very well for about 80 years until she could no longer remember the year! She was always known as Jeanne. Why she had this French name when none of her family seemed to have any French connection, is a mystery. My father, Frank Bell Cooper was born on 21 January 1920, just 13 days later. At the time of their birth, it would have seemed highly unlikely that these two people would meet and marry and live in Australia. But as has often been said, the war changed all that!

My mother was born in London and grew up in Essex, to the North East of the city, in a village called Chigwell. She was the third daughter after sisters known as Bunty (real name Joyce Kathleen) and Sally (Doreen). The three girls were followed by a much-wanted son, who was named James. Sadly, he had

Down syndrome and lived, as far as I know, most of his life with a woman who cared for him in her home. He was not hidden away, however, as I clearly remember being taken to visit him as a teenager.

My mother's parents were Charles Lovett and Annie Maude (née Hine). My English cousin has told me that Charles was not a well-off fellow but was enterprising and while still a young lad, started to fix people's bicycles. He did well it seems and went on to make cars at a time when they were first being built. When WWII broke out, he was required to stay home and make motorcycles for the war. I am told Annie was from a more 'well-to-do family'. I met her and remember her well as a small but elegantly dressed, very British lady, who seemed less conventional than my mother. Charles must have done very well as, it seems from the beginning, and they lived in a huge, square house in Essex, known as The Grange, with servants and a gardener. The latter's name was Broad and he came each day on a bicycle and was given bread and dripping at lunchtime, which I trust was just some extra treat! He would have been needed, as behind the large garden were vegetable plots and an orchard. That is just how it was then. People grew a lot of their own food out the back! Later, the depression hit and the servants had to go and they moved, I believe, to a smaller house in the area.

My mother went to a secondary school called Felixstowe Ladies College, which was on the coast, not very far from her home, but she was a boarder there.

As a child, my mother and her sister, Sally, went to ballet lessons and my mother became very keen on it. At a time when few women thought of a career, by the age of nineteen, she was dancing at Covent Garden. She told me she danced in Swan Lake, and sometimes she performed the role of one of the four cygnets, which is a very difficult dance as the arms are locked together with the three other dancers. She laughed when she told me that her father was against her career to start with and her mother had to persuade him that their daughter was not 'on the boards' in the 'common' sense! Her young life was very happy I think. The whole family was very keen on tennis and they had lots of social life with local families and their young men.

Then the war broke out and that was the end of the ballet. Mum and my Aunt Sally joined up together into the Women's Auxiliary Air Force (WAAF). (I am not aware of her sister Bunty's movements then.) They were asked what they could do. Sally said typewriting, so she was given a job using that and my mother had done a first aid course, and was given something vaguely related, but it was all pretty ad hoc. Ultimately, my mother was a personnel officer and in charge of the welfare of WAAF officers on Air Force stations.

Jeanne as a young woman in England

When posted to a Royal Air Force station called Kirton in Lindsey in Lincolnshire, she met my father, an Australian from Victoria, who technically, although a qualified pilot of Spitfires and Hurricanes, ranked below her for a while. On her arrival, he apparently asked, "Who is the new Queen Bee?" which I believe referred to the personnel officer in charge of the women on the station. The fact that she had briefly out-ranked him became a perennial family joke, because she was, after all, just a woman!

My father was one of the lucky ones who survived the war as a fighter pilot, having flown from late 1942 to the end of the war. Like many couples in England, they married in August 1945. By the time my father was finally discharged from service on 28 February 1946, my mother was on a 'bride ship' to Australia already pregnant with me.

My conception after only six weeks of marriage and prior to leaving for Australia was, of course, a disaster at that time and, understandably very traumatic for them both. My birth so early in their marriage must have been a difficult start and a strain for my mother when arriving in a new country. She went first to Frank's mother's house in Croydon, outside Melbourne, until he returned. This must have been a considerable change for her, if not a shock. Australia was a very different culture from England in those days.

They lived in Croydon until a friend found them a flat in the city, which were extremely hard to come by at the time. My father was able to study for an Arts degree through the returned servicemen's scheme. This would not have been easy with a baby in a small flat. There was, however, a nice garden for me to play in, and my mother had support from another resident in the small block that looked after me. I might have been better off with her, as one day my mother took me shopping and returned with the feeling she had left something behind. She had left me in my pram outside the butcher's! She was obviously distracted and I think these were difficult days in some ways.

My mother's sister said my father never forgave me for being born and held similar views as the years went on. I have no memory of him at this time, but his sister and his mother said that he would one day regret the way he treated me as a small child. I doubt that he ever did. He grew into a difficult personality and we did not stand up to him. I don't think anyone did!

Subsequently, my father joined the Public Service, which for him involved further training, which he somehow had to do while finishing his degree. After four years in Melbourne, they left for London for three years and chose to live in Chigwell again. After a further two years in Bonn, they returned and made Canberra their permanent home. My mother liked Canberra well enough and did not seem to miss England very much. Certainly in later years, she would report after various visits back there to her sisters, that England was so changed anyway that there was little left to miss. She was happy to become an Australian in reality, although she never sought official citizenship.

My mother was outwardly a warm person, but seemed closed off from her relationships. She was a good mother in the dutiful sense, but I never knew what she was really thinking. I never saw her show any form of emotion, even on the death of my father, that is, until one day at the end of her life when she had lost those inhibitions due to dementia. She simply believed that showing emotion was not 'done', so she didn't! Her behaviour was very governed by the conventions of her culture and, I would say, sharpened by the 'stiff upper lip' that was required during the war years, when she was in her early twenties. I think this social 'requirement' would have had a significant and lasting effect on her personal development.

My mother sometimes talked wistfully of the war, even though she had had an earlier fiancé who died, and she would have known losses of loved ones and friends. Her sister, Sally, lost her first husband, who was also a pilot, but she subsequently remarried and was happy. However, the war itself brought people together in a way that was exciting for courageous young people. This is not hard to imagine. Everything was sharpened and clear. Good times seemed like magic and relationships far more romantic than under other circumstances. I wish I had been told more of her wartime experience.

The awful experience of losing people in war was of course also true for my father, but I suspect he had to bear the losses of close friends and colleagues more often and more keenly. His war started with the death of his best friend, Arthur with whom he had enlisted, left Australia, trained and sailed to the UK. I think he died on his first sortie out and my father wrote in his diary: 'I don't know how I will go on without him'. Not something I would ever hear my father say in later life. I believe he was different then and clearly recorded his distress at losing his companion, and also his loneliness at other times. There had also been the loss of another pilot, Peter, who had been a best friend from home. The day Arthur died, my father also wrote: 'First Peter, then Arthur, curse the bloody war'. And so, it went on. One only has to think of losing one's sibling or best friend now. They were no different then, but they just had to get on with it the next day.

I don't think it is possible to have such experiences without suffering considerable trauma, which ultimately never goes away. I think that the physical effects on the body and on the psyche would have been accumulative and debilitating. And at the end of it all, those who survived, must have wondered and questioned why they were still alive when others were not. I think this would inevitably have resulted in what has been called 'survivor guilt syndrome'. In my father's case, he must have questioned: Why did he go on to marry the gorgeous wife, and have a family, and a successful career, and good health, until a reasonable old age?

Those comrades whom he lost never knew any of those things. So, when I said he was one of the lucky ones, this must have been, in one sense, almost a heavy burden to bear. Would one question actions in a given situation and wonder how another might have done it? Would one question whether one was brave enough, or dedicated enough? All those serving would have seen intense heroism and sacrifice from some of those around them. Would one look back on that and wonder why some even saved many others by their own sacrifice, whether deliberately or unwittingly? Did my father have any reason to question himself? I have no idea, but I doubt it. The questioning would be there in the mind anyway, I suspect. Probably forever.

Tennis finals with her mother and friends

From all accounts, my father was a positive personality and good fun when he was young, and even during the war, and immediately after it. His family and friends never said anything else. But I think his personality progressively changed due to what we now know as post-traumatic stress. How could he have stayed the same? While he became increasingly adept at presenting his public persona, he became increasingly unable to present himself to his wife and family at home. As the years went on, he became implacably morose. This was not a mood, but a permanent state. However, if friends came to the house and when he was out, a charming smile would emerge as if from nowhere and I would think: Who is that? How different he looks!

My father seemed to lose his respect for women, but maybe that was just the norm then. He made my mother feel a fool at times in front of me, so I can imagine how it might have been in private. His anger was often quite irrational. My being born a girl would not have helped and when I was seven and my brother, Paul, was on the way, I prayed that he would be a boy as then we would all be able to survive better. Another girl and we were sunk! I remember the amazingly boyish grin on my father's face in the light from the corridor outside my bedroom door, when he woke me to tell me, "It's a boy!" I find it odd now that I was not invited to get up out of bed and join him. At the time, I simply lay back on the pillow and thanked God for the right outcome!

My mother was no fool and while she put up with my father's behaviour, she did it largely by the use of silence. This was partly to protect the children no doubt, but also as a way of not engaging in something she must have known she could not change. He had the job, the money, the social position (which was important to my mother) and he had fought in the war. And she was dependent on him for everything.

I think my mother suffered from a sense of disappointment, as she slid into the role of wife and mother. She lost the independence and sense of identity which must have been enhanced during her time as a dancer, in her war service, and in early social relationships. Much later, she mentioned that she was considering getting a job. *Perhaps in a library*, she thought. Privately, I knew how hard it would be at the time in the 1980s when jobs were short and my mother was not trained. The idea of a job never came to anything, but she must have thought about it at length prior to saying anything. I know a friend of hers in very similar circumstances also considered a job, but did not ultimately try to get one. Her daughter joked to me about this once.

My parents frequently used to use the word 'girl' for secretarial worker and other junior female office staff. They used to pronounce it long and very pejoratively, the implication being that these people were intractably stupid. It seemed worse when my mother used this term to somehow elevate herself above these working women, which showed her real need to give herself status as a 'wife'. I just thought, *She could not do such jobs herself!*

When I finished school, they sent me off to secretarial school to become someone's 'girl'. As I could not suggest something else acceptable to them, I could not really complain. It was too late for dancer, or ice-skater, and anything else would have sounded like a money drain to them. I loathed it, and was belittled and crushed by it, especially as all my friends were at university. However, the skills stood me in good stead and I eventually managed to lift myself out of that role. But my mother, being at home, never had that opportunity to improve herself in a way that could have provided her with a new sense of identity.

After her success as a dancer, in married life, she had no goals of her own, which must have been a difficult mental shift. Her interests were playing the piano, which she had learnt as a child and eventually took up again including lessons in Canberra. I think playing it took her back to her youth. For a while, she made tapestry cushions and stool covers. She also studied language books for new postings away and sometimes attended classes as well. She certainly acquired a working level of German. When I was seventeen, she made my clothes for parties. They were very well made, although while she tried to do what I wanted, they were a bit her version of it and not really 'cool'. But I was grateful for her efforts to dress me well.

Social life, while she was good at it, became increasingly a huge strain for someone who was an introvert by nature and who said she felt, wrongly I think, unable to identify things that she had done that were interesting to others. She certainly always managed to be very gracious to everyone she encountered. She also had a lively sense of humour. She used to play tennis, but stopped going, as she just seemed to prefer to stay at home. She simply found it difficult to find something to say, so it was hard work and tiring. And yet, I have the feeling that this should not have been the case at all. I always thought that she could have been quite different, and I think she did too. I think the heavy atmosphere in her home brought about by my father's constant tetchiness and frequent tempers, left her feeling exhausted and that any plans of her own seemed futile.

I know my mother blamed my father for 'taking it out on the kids when he came home from the office', mainly because she actually said so, which was very unlike her. I don't suppose this was unusual, and I think men had such a burden of responsibility in those days being the only breadwinner, that stress was a common result. He worked selflessly to provide the best for his family and spent little on himself.

When my brother and I were older and leaving school, family discussion and resources were channelled to my brother and his career. I had been expected to fend for myself after some initial training, which was far from a complete year, in typing and shorthand. I think that strategy was to encourage girls to find someone to marry and be 'off the family books'! I heard that from other young women at the time. Eventually, it became clear that I could get all that for myself anyway thanks! Our generation of women who were lucky enough to have been given a good education, as I was, were able to gain an early independence.

It may have been threatening for our mothers to have daughters who did not follow the same life pattern of wife and mother without paid work outside the home. I am guilty of having had disregard for that kind of life when I was young. I never expressed the view that my mother should have done otherwise, but the obvious changes going on among the feminist generation, which became the new norm, may well have rankled, or even undermined our mothers' confidence. Their own youth was taken away by the war in more ways than one. My mother's career, for example, could not be resurrected. Not that that was her goal, having married by then and left London, but the war had taken away the choice. In many ways, my father's job was a job for a couple and my mother engaged in that as much as she was required to. My father said on a couple of occasions that he could not have done it without her, and I am confident he meant it. My mother did like being the wife of somebody working for the government. Almost all their friends were from the same Department, with the clear exception of a family who lived near us in our first home in Yarralumla, Canberra, whose company I preferred.

My mother also needed security. I think this was paramount for her. And my father once said that marriage gave his life structure. So, I think the marriage worked out of mutual need. However, moral support only seemed to go one way, and certainly did not extend to me. My brother on the other hand, did have support in many forms. His approach to family was, as a result, different from mine, although he did not have an easy time either, and he too was aware of the constant tensions.

My mother was a person given to acquiescence by nature. Girls were perhaps brought up then to comply, rather than stand up for themselves. Or perhaps it was just my father who left her feeling powerless. I know I felt let down by her in never standing up for herself and for us children against my father, especially when he was blatantly wrong in his judgement. It always felt like a double betrayal because she always kept silent.

In later years, to his great credit, my father said, "I fought a gentleman's war," and was self-effacing about his whole role in it. He meant that he was flying and shooting down enemy pilots one night, and may literally be dining at The Ritz the next. He was conscious that those in the Army or at sea were there for the duration. There was no relief for them. No bath and a meal in the Mess after a night's battle. But my father thought he was not a physically strong man, and so decided flying would be the best choice for him. Of course, nobody fought an easy war, and I know he was roughing it in a tent in France for a while. In any event, the very knowledge that the following night, instead of enjoying a meal, he may be shot down, must surely have become one long screeching, nerve-wracking roller coaster.

It is clear that the war had a huge effect on all those involved and that the effect lasted longer than one generation. If only it had been understood that basic counselling was needed to at least unlock any doubt and guilt so that the person could put things in some perspective and begin to build a positive future. They at least needed to be convinced that they were in no way responsible, not for their actions while fighting, and not for surviving. They had just given it their all, but the very fact that it was impossible to talk about it, simply compounded the situation for most of them. It has always seemed to me that to talk about it would have caused them to show emotion, and that was not something they wanted to do in front of anyone. They were brought up not to, and then they were trained never to.

One of the saddest things is the lack of awareness of my generation about what actually happened to our parents, and the effect those events had on them. I feel keenly that I should have asked more about the war. My brother did talk with my father about the war as a child, but it would not have reflected the reality. Like most boys, he played with soldiers and made model aeroplanes. I think my father was happy that he took such an interest, but it was very much a game to a child. I wonder what my father really felt watching those games. I would have thought, *And so on, and so forth...*

Before my father died aged almost 80, my mother already showed signs of dementia which would vary in intensity. For a while after he died, she was not clear in her mind at all, and her memory was significantly diminished. However, within a short time, she seemed to get a new lease on life and appeared to have short term plans for playing music and not having television on in the evening. She seemed to be realising that she was now free and had control of her whole house and garden.

We bought her an easy sound system to play CDs, but unfortunately, her mind never did quite manage it. This period of energy was short lived unfortunately, but she and I did have a very good year or so, in a way which we had not before. We did a lot of things together and at that time, my mother was able to enjoy social settings, but most of all, she loved going to movies on Sunday afternoons.

With time, when her dementia worsened and she could no longer remember what year it was, let alone her own age, we engaged a 'helper', who was invaluable. I had thought I could never work again, as she needed a lot of help during the day. She had a great relationship with her helper and was very fond of her I think. We were very lucky to have such a dedicated person.

Eventually, my mother went into a high care home in Sydney near my brother and his family. This was partly because we could not find a care home in Canberra that suited us, but also because my brother and his wife thought I had done the caring to this point and that they could now take over. This was very kind of them. It was a lot of work for my sister-in-law, who was wonderful in stepping up to what I called the 'pointy end' of aged care. Sometimes when my mother's health seemed to be going downhill, I would go up to Sydney and stay with the family and go to her each mealtime and get her to eat. All it took really was for her to see her own child and she would come good again and after a few days, I would go home. One time, she was in hospital and I arrived and saw this tiny grey-coloured woman slumped in a chair by her hospital bed. As she saw me, her face was incredulous and she smiled and was so pleased she was not alone after all. After a few minutes, she said to me, "I have been so frightened." And with that, she broke into tears briefly, which was the only time I saw emotion on her face. In a way that was good thing, as it showed me that she was just like us all really, when she was no longer aware enough to act otherwise. By the time I left late that afternoon, she had regained all her colour and was physically and mentally a different person. By the end of the week, she was able to return to the care home, although I think she thought she was returning to her family home in England!

My brother always had a great relationship with our mother, and his son was her only grandchild. However, he looked so much like my brother at that age that when he visited her, I think my mother thought she was talking to her son a lot of the time! So that proved to be a good way for her to end her days. I would visit for the day or for longer from Canberra. Most of the time she knew who I was, but occasionally, I became my Aunt Sally in England. This was fine with me as I liked my Aunt Sally very much, and I knew they had got on very well as sisters! Sometimes she would not realise that she was no longer in England and would ask how everyone at the house was. By this, she meant her childhood home.

At this time, it was still possible to have an enjoyable conversation in the present. If she slipped back into her early life, I would joke and say something like 'Look out the window at that bright sunshine. That is Australia out there, not England, isn't it?' I would remind her that she moved here, and she would laugh and the issue would be forgotten. But sadly, she had no memory at all of the house we lived in for forty odd years in Charlotte Street in Canberra, even though she had photos of it. Other photos also meant nothing to her anymore. I think she was aware that she had forgotten her life, and so often the framed photos that my sister-in-law had produced for her, would be stacked up, upside down on the window shelf where they had been displayed, presumably so that she would not be reminded of what was now irretrievable to her.

My mother survived to her 90th birthday and as I had just visited, I left that day to my brother to do, who took her a cake. All I said to him was, "Don't tell her she is ninety," as she once said to me, incredulously, that 'so and so' had lived to eighty, and repeated herself 'imagine eighty'! So better not to tell her that she was ninety!

The week before my mother died, I had visited her and the family for three days. I last saw her walking in to lunch in the care home. When I drove back at the end of that week, I missed her death by half an hour. I would have to say that this made it easier for me, and made no difference to her, as she was unconscious and had not been aware of her situation at all. My brother sat with her. I don't know how he did that, but I was very grateful that he had had the courage.

Possibly the saddest thing I would note about my parents was that I don't recall them being particularly happy about anything. They seemed to live out their lives under a sense of 'duty'. It was a word they had used. Those of us lucky to be brought up with a sense of discipline are likely to use this facility for the rest of our lives. Perhaps the pressure of duty was also a legacy of the war and proved to be hard to shake. But I don't think they started out that way. They were not like that when they married. Being parents and working is hard enough, but I think that generation, increasingly as years went by, also had to overcome their war experience like some ever-shifting platform under their feet. Perhaps they slowly accepted that survival to do one's duty may be enough, or in fact, all they could manage. If we cannot stop wars, we must at least recognise that they do not end for the participants when they are over, and that maybe for many, their war never really ends at all.

One could question whether that generation of women had an experience that was preferable to the one before when women were even more limited in their options. My grandmother was a lively sort of woman, who I am told, loved parties and travel. But there was never any option other than to be married and have children. At least the war generation had some choices and probably acute awareness of alternatives and personal options, even though they were encouraged to abandon them after the war. Some generations have things that bind them as a group and the war certainly did that. It also provided a common understanding of pulling through tough times and contributing one's best. A friend of my mother's said to me recently, "We had to be supportive women, so that they could be heroes." Later, on reflection, I accepted that was how it was. That view might not sound like 'equality' to subsequent generations, but surely, they all were heroes, and who are we to question how they did it?

Chapter 14

Hilda Corson Simpson (Née Rodgers)

Vee Saunders

Vee and I met in the library at ANU in 1964; she was extraordinarily helpful when one struggled to find one's way through the non-computerised library catalogue card system. Vee had had an amazingly thrilling life, or so it seemed to me, someone who had hardly left Canberra. She was born in Benghazi but Scottish by ancestry, her father a judge and she had been at boarding school in Scotland. We soon became friends and saw a lot of one another as our friend, Denis Saunders, seemed to be unable to do anything without her and she joined our group activities. Vee loved to write and read but by 1968, she and Denis were married and off to Western Australia where she became as devoted a bird bander as he was. We attended parties at Vee's house while we were together at ANU and her very stylish mother presided over the affairs.

Robbie Henderson

Determination as substantial as the granite hills that form the backbone of her native land, Scotland, drove Hilda, my mother. She was an unstoppable force, a true-blue stocking, intelligent and elegant, yet petite sometimes physically frail and proudly Scottish. No matter where she went and what she did, she never lost either her deep love for Scotland or her soft brogue.

The elements which shaped her were historic and psychological. She was powered by nervous energy; she simply couldn't sit still. She was born with all the advantages of being a Scot, and having being born in Dundee. Being a Scot is relevant to her story because, before any other country in Britain, several centuries before my mother's birth, Scotland had recognised the value of good education. From 1560, the Church of Scotland, the national church, introduced universal education, providing a university-educated 'dominie' or teacher in every parish. Scotland's four ancient universities, St Andrews, Glasgow, Aberdeen and Edinburgh are among the oldest in Britain. When Hilda was born in 1914, Dundee was only just beginning to decline as one of the most affluent industrial cities in the United Kingdom, known for the three Js—jute, journalism and jam. It was also the site of a successful whaling industry which provided the oil essential for the vast factory machines. One imagines a bustling, reeking city where unemployment was rare and 70% of women were employed. Hilda's father was Managing Director of Baxters, one of the biggest jute companies in the city. I don't think directors in those days had the outrageous incomes to which they feel entitled today, but I am certain that my mother's family enjoyed a comfortable middle-class life.

A good education in the Scottish tradition at Morgan Academy, a fee-paying co-ed school prepared my mother well for entry to St Andrews University where she studied Arts. Almost obligatory to an Arts degree course at St Andrews were Latin, Philosophy and a science subject. It was in her Philosophy class in 1933 that she met my father and later, married him in December 1941. She always referred to their relationship as 'the marriage of true minds', a quote from one of Shakespeare's sonnets. In Dad's memoirs, he described his first sight of a frivolous bejantine (first year female student) 'talking animatedly and laughing with fellow students'.

Hilda majored in both French and English (including Anglo Saxon) language and literature, winning the English medal two years in a row. Of course, an energetic thinking young woman like my mother couldn't resist the pull of university politics, becoming the first-year student representative on the Students' Representative Council. In her own words, this made her feel 'at the heart of university life'. Although all of this may seem superficial and unnecessary, these are the initial sketches preparatory to the full portrait of my mother.

Being a French scholar, she had the opportunity to study at the Sorbonne and looked back on this time in France, Paris and the Loire Valley with great fondness. In truth, Mum could be said to be more French than the French! She would insist on speaking in French to my father and me, becoming peeved and look pained when we would reply in English! In 1938, she spent the summer on a scholarship in Geneva at the League of Nations Summer School of International Relations.

Hilda as a student at the University of St Andrews in 1933. The students at St Andrews wore and still wear scarlet gowns.

Her experiences in Geneva led Hilda to consider a career in journalism as a foreign correspondent. With Europe teetering on the brink of war, no paper would take on a woman in that capacity, the international situation was too fragile and it was probably considered an unsuitable career for a woman. Little did they know my mother! It was probably the only time in her life when she couldn't do exactly as she wanted! However, with that door slammed in her face, Hilda decided to teach. In 1940, she accepted a post at Duke of Gordon's Secondary School in Huntly, north of Dundee in Aberdeenshire. Teaching posts became more available as young men joined the military forces as a result of the outbreak of the Second World War. In 1941, this facilitated a move back to a teaching position in Dundee to join her parents. Hilda was never in the armed forces but, aside from her teaching, was involved in several voluntary roles which were an integral part of wartime Britain. On several occasions, she helped escort evacuee children to the station in Dundee, not a task she would have cherished having limited tolerance of children! Dundee and the immediate area only suffered one air raid unlike more strategic ports further north like Fraserburgh and Aberdeen.

Polish airmen and other servicemen were forced to escape to Britain when Poland was overrun by the Nazis. In Dundee, a Scottish-Polish Club was set up, mainly as a social outlet for these exiled men, far from family and friends. Being a gifted linguist, she enthusiastically threw herself into adding Polish to her repertoire of languages. Apparently, she was fluent in a very short time thanks to her ear for language. Being the social butterfly that she was, Hilda enjoyed organising functions such as dances and other social events. Learning of any kind was such a pleasure to her.

As others collect china or glassware, my mother collected languages and was frequently acquiring yet another one. She was already fluent in French, later she spoke fluent Italian, Malay and Swahili. In the 1960s, before a holiday to Yugoslavia, she managed to make herself understood in Serbo-Croat and had a smattering of useful Arab words from her time in Cyrenaica where she lived after the war ended.

My father had joined the British Army in 1939 at the outbreak of war, not waiting to be called up. In December 1941, my parents married in Dundee. Within days of their marriage, Dad received word of an immediate posting to the Middle East, which cut short their honeymoon. It would be three and a half years before they were together again. I know that my mother missed Dad badly, but she absorbed herself in her job and the many other activities which she enthusiastically threw herself into. Apart from that single air raid in Dundee, which did little damage and being in the midst of one in London, she seemed relatively unscathed by the more violent aspects of wartime Britain. Her memoirs refer to a visit to Bristol to see her younger sister Kathleen, who was a radar operator in the WAAF, having given up her studies at the Royal Academy of Music to serve in the armed forces. While walking down the street, Kathleen fainted from tension and sheer exhaustion, but was unable to tell Mum why, such was the secret nature of her job. Mum's mind churned with the concern that her younger sister, Kathleen, was under such stress. Not long after, Kathleen suffered a nervous breakdown. As far as Mum could guess, this seemed to coincide with the build-up for the Normandy landings.

Dad spent most of the war in the Middle East, in Egypt, Lebanon and Palestine with time in Saudi Arabia. His musical ear also gave him a gift for languages, soon making him fluent in Arabic. After a brief leave in Scotland after the war, my father, still an army officer was appointed Custodian of Enemy Property in Cyrenaica (now part of Libya) in the British Military Administration. His understanding and fluency in Arabic, plus his experiences in the Middle East undoubtedly led to this posting.

Hilda on her wedding day in Dundee 30 December 1941.
Clothing rations in UK in 1941 meant that Hilda wore the same wedding dress her sister had worn a few years earlier.

It was in Benghazi, Cyrenaica, my mother joined him and where I was born. Here in the former Italian colony, with its quasi-colonial lifestyle, my parents conceived the idea of joining the British Colonial Service when my Dad went back into civilian life. Knowing my mother's ambition, she was almost certainly the impetus behind this plan. Years later, my father told me that he had imagined a quiet life as a country solicitor in Crieff, Scotland, he'd reckoned without the dynamo, my mother! They were complete opposites; he was quiet, unassuming and gentle but occasionally showed a dry Scottish wit. It was he who wrote the weekly aerogrammes to me, their only child, back at boarding school on the cold, windy east coast of Scotland.

In 1948, my parents and I went to Singapore; my father had been appointed as Crown Counsel and Deputy Public Prosecutor. Wives in the British colonies in the 1950s didn't work. It simply wasn't done! However apart from her time in Cyrenaica, Hilda had always worked and was undeterred by this. She had soon applied for and been appointed as head of the English department of Singapore Teachers' Training College. Despite being the department head, despite her qualifications as a married woman, she was not entitled to any increments for past experience, or a pension and her long leaves to Britain every three years were unpaid. So much did she love working, these were the conditions she accepted. I suspect that it removed her from her more awkward maternal duties, given that I had an amah to look after me.

A photo of Hilda taken in Singapore in the 1950s—taken at a friend's house.

In her eyes, motherhood was not her primary role; her career came first. Teaching aside, one of my mother's major achievements in Singapore was writing textbooks on teaching English as a Second Language. She wrote 'A Comprehensive Study in Spoken English' with both a student's and a teacher's text and edited an anthology of poetry for junior and senior schools. Royalties from the 'Spoken English' books continued to roll in for several years after her death in 1999. Evidently, the books were very popular in India!

Life in the various colonial posts meant my parents employed servants to fulfil various roles, such as cook, amah and a couple of gardeners. My mother would talk of gardening, but for her it consisted merely of picking the roses! Even if the Raj was gasping its final breaths, it helped mould and refine the woman my mother became. Hilda was away from home during the day teaching. In the tropical evenings, my parent socialised with friends, went Scottish country dancing at the Burns Club, or my mother was in the throes of rehearsals for yet another drama extravaganza. Fred in the meantime, had been asked to redraft the laws of Singapore and was incredibly busy with that task. Luckily, our servants, including Ah Woon my amah, looked after me very well. Often I would eat with the cook's family in the servants' quarters while my parents were busy elsewhere.

Her role in life was as the star attraction; my mother always preferred centre stage. Theatre in its many forms enthralled her. Loved, respected and admired by her students, every year she would throw herself into producing plays and Gilbert and Sullivan operettas with her Chinese, Indian and Malay students taking on principal roles or singing in the chorus. It was a tribute to her skills and vast imagination as a producer that the Gilbert and Sullivan productions were held in the Victoria Theatre in Singapore, the largest theatre on the island. She was equally involved in theatre in Ghana where, in 1956, she and Fred went to live for five years. In Accra, the capital city, she produced 'Julius Caesar' with a predominantly Ghanaian cast. In Sarawak and Sabah, she also produced plays or pageants. Perhaps that's where her true vocation lay, maybe she should have chosen a career in acting, she certainly loved the limelight!

Throughout their working lives, my parents remained very British in their outlook, concerned with the formal structure and culture of life in the outposts of Empire. My mother in particular was a stickler for what she considered the necessary protocol; who took precedence at social functions because there was a very definite hierarchy. In fact, a week before my mother died, high on pethidine and hallucinating, she held a very formal tea party in her private room in hospital. The visitors and nurses were all aware that Hilda was 'away with the pixies' and played their roles. Hilda hosted the party, waved regally to indicate where they should sit. Guests were introduced to each other and offered cakes and Indian or China tea!

Despite their Britishness and formality, both of my parents were unconventional in their choice of friends and my school, and in the treatment of our servants. Mum and Dad moved in many social circles, but unlike the other British people in Singapore, they had Chinese, Indian, Ceylonese (Sri Lankan) and Malay friends. Raffles Girls' School, where I started my education was not a British school; in fact, there were four British girls at the school when I was there. I'm certain that this was my mother's influence at work, a deliberate ploy to teach me to embrace diversity. It saddened me in their later years that they became racist.

It was in Kenya that the change in attitude emerged, fuelled by the intolerant attitude among white settlers who saw the end of their era in Africa, despite being born and raised there.

I hesitate to mark World War 2 as a major component in shaping of Hilda. It is possible that, but for the war, she may not have landed a teaching job at the Duke of Gordon's School in Huntly. Nevertheless, I suspect that she would have talked her way into that position; she was very voluble and persuasive! Some people may claim that it was only as the men marched off to war that jobs for women became more readily available. The force that drove her would not have countenanced a life without using her intellect of which she was extremely proud and at pains to demonstrate. I've cringed on occasion as she sought to correct facts or correct a French pronunciation! Despite her own accomplishments, she was immensely ambitious for Dad and unfailingly supportive, as he was of her career. Fred ended his long legal career as Chief Justice of Kenya. As a result, he was dubbed Knight Bachelor by Her Majesty Queen Elizabeth in 1985. His title meant so much more to her than to him, she cherished her title and used it whenever possible.

On leaving Heathrow after my father's investiture at Buckingham Palace, my mother asked whether they could go into the VIP lounge as usual. Imagine her horror when the British Airways ground staff told her that it was occupied, not only occupied but by members of a pop group! Mother was incensed! I remember hearing her make a hairdressing appointment and starting the phone conversation with 'Lady Simpson here'. I was so embarrassed. Why couldn't she say 'Hilda here'? Why did she need to be so pompous? Accolades, degrees and titles, whatever their form delighted her, even my husband Denis' honours degree in Zoology and subsequent Doctorate! Her greatest disappointment was that I, her only child, didn't emulate her, didn't choose the academic life. She could never understand why I chose the role of wife and mother, over the possibility of a degree and a career. She failed to understand that I had deliberately chosen a different path from hers, having missed her, and resented her career and her total absorption in a life which allowed little time for motherhood. What she had taught me by default was that motherhood was an important role in itself; in fact, if one chose to be a mother, it was a role to embrace rather than neglect.

Hilda was not without her humorous side. Not only did she have a sense of humour, despite her pretentiousness, she could laugh at herself. When learning Bahasa Melayu (Malay), she was naturally anxious to practise her new language. We used to go to the Singapore Swimming Club every Sunday morning. One Sunday morning, early in the learning process, we arrived at the gates of the club. Being polite, she greeted the very portly Sikh doorman, "*Salamat pagi* (good morning), *gaja*." His jaw dropped and he stepped back a few paces, but recovered quickly, doubling up with laughter! It only took a few moments to realise that instead of calling him '*jaga*' or guard, she had called him '*gaja*' or elephant! She dined out on this story for years!

In the 1950s, while she was on the staff at Singapore Teachers' Training College, I was allowed to go to one of the College's swimming galas. Hilda was near the edge of the pool, elegantly dressed in hat, gloves, stylish polka dot dress and high heels when a student dashed out of the crowd and pushed her into the pool. I was furious that he should be so bold. I ran towards the front of the crowd protesting at her treatment. My ruffled feathers were quickly smoothed, the tears wiped away. The whole episode was a set-up, a planned comic act to add some levity to the day's programme.

The road my mother trod was entirely of her choosing. I don't believe that anything or anyone could divert her from that route, certainly not World War 2. I have to confess to a grudging admiration of her steely sense of purpose, her unwavering self-confidence. There were no obstacles which couldn't be kicked aside or climbed over. The only times I ever saw her disconcerted were when the conversation didn't relate to her or the topic was not within her grasp. She would then change the topic to one related to her own exploits. She became adept at this but we could soon predict when she was about to pounce!

Despite admiring her achievements, I can't ignore the scars I bear as a result of her spitefulness, her criticism and her all-too-evident disappointment in her only child. I failed to measure up to her and that was my failing. For all her achievements, Hilda had done the conventional thing in having a child but that child had let her down. I mention this because it is the flip side of the indomitable force that my mother was; worshipped by Fred, the life and soul of every party, the evergreen academic, and the 'frivolous bejantine' even in her later years.

Chapter 15

Joyce Margaret Hartnell (Née Webster)

Marg Furnell

Marg came to CCEGGS in the middle years of high school and soon became a part of the friendship group with CGS. Her house was conveniently located midway between the schools on Mugga Way and it was not long before it became a stopping off point for us as we rode to and from school. Mrs Hartnell was usually there ensuring we all behaved ourselves.

Marg was very good at languages especially French, so it was no surprise when she became a Qantas hostess on their international route after leaving school. She was also a very good tennis player as was Geoff Furnell, Denis Saunders's best friend, and they occasionally played one another. It was not until they were approaching 70 years of age that they finally married.

Robbie Henderson

Joyce (or Joy as she preferred later—always Web to her closest friends), was born in Stratford, Gippsland, Victoria May 2 1919 to Tom and Ella Webster. Joy had three brothers, Geoff, John and Norman. They lived an idyllic early life in the Victorian countryside at 'Craigielea' and later all went to boarding school in Geelong. Mum to the Hermitage in 1932, and the boys to Geelong College. Joy's main love during those years was horse riding and socialising.

My grandfather did not want my mother to go to university, as she would have liked to do—instead she was sent to a finishing school called Invergowrie also in Geelong (her parents felt it was important to become a lady). Following her graduation from Invergowrie, she joined the Victorian Electricity Commission as a cooking demonstrator. Very apt for a young 'lady'!

Joy was very influenced by the depression of the 1930s, as she was on the farm with her parents through most of it. She told of large numbers of itinerant men with swags who used to turn up looking for a job and a feed. Apparently, her parents never turned anyone away. They would always find something for the men to do to qualify for at least a meal. She could never understand why so many of them came to 'Craigielea'. She later found out that someone had carved into the front gatepost a symbol known to itinerant men that they would be looked after at that address.

Joy and her mother and brother on the farm at Stratford

My mother with the three children

Joy at boarding school on left

As was the norm in those days especially in the country, most social gatherings were at home. This is where, in the late 1930s, she met a shy young Air Force officer by the name of Geoffrey Hartnell. He was staying with his cousins in Sale which was not far from Stratford. Following a short courtship, they married in Melbourne at All Saints Church (corner of Punt and Toorak Rd) on the 9 June 1941. During World War 2, Geoff was posted to Cairns/Townsville as the CO 20 Squadron Catalinas, on convoy escort in the Coral Sea, and night operations in the Bismarck Sea against the Japanese, from late 1942 to February 1943. Joy was in Townsville with Geoff.

Geoff returned to Melbourne to the Air Force Headquarters in St Kilda and in March 1943 was posted as CO 10 Squadron UK engaged in anti-submarine patrols in the Bay of Biscay. Joy returned to her parent's home, pregnant, and was there for the remainder of the war. During the war, Joy did a lot of volunteer work (which continued throughout her life) and assisted her parents on the farm. Anthony Geoffrey (Tony) was born in June 1943; a few months after Geoff was posted to the UK.

After the war, times were tough for everyone—wives had become resilient and quite innovative while their partners were away and I remember this continuing throughout my early childhood. Second-hand or homemade goods were common. I was told that early in the 1950s Qantas Airways approached my father and asked him to join them as a captain. My mother was horrified and said it was too fledgling a company and the Air Force was far more stable! Dad did what he was told.

My mother's time alone during the war had certainly made her a lot stronger and a force to be reckoned with. During the war, Geoffrey wrote to Joy and his mother every day. This gave all of his family a huge insight into his life during the war as it had Joy and had helped enormously to cope with her life back in Australia.

Geoffrey came back from England at the end of World War 2 to East Sale as Commanding Officer and my parents were reunited. Tony was introduced to his father. In 1946, they all moved as a family to the RAAF Base Pearce near Perth where Dad was CO. Joy was pregnant again with her second child. Margaret was born in Perth in 1946. A more subdued, placid version of her older brother!

For the next 20 odd years, the Hartnells were constantly on the move. Joy thrived on the different postings. Her personality and earlier training certainly made the never-ending social commitments easier for the more retiring Geoffrey. He often said he could not have done it without her.

From Pearce WA, Geoffrey became Director Intelligence Air Force Headquarters in St Kilda, Vic. 1949–50. The third child, Ian David, was born in 1948; the apple of his mother's eye.

Geoffrey was Commanding Officer Base Squadron Point Cook from July 1950 to November 1951 and CO Amberley Qld November 1951–52. It was a new RAAF Base and Joy was instrumental in the start-up of a new kindergarten—it became very successful and is still to this day.

Following Amberley, Geoffrey was sent to Operational Command Headquarters at Glenbrook in the Blue Mountains, NSW for approximately three years. There was a major bush fire which almost decimated homes on the Base but luckily, the wind changed at the last minute. Joy was home alone at the time and single handed calmly packed as many things as she could into the car just in case!

Melbourne followed again, the children stayed at school and Geoff and Joy went to Butterworth Base in Malaysia; Geoff as the CO. Joy loved having staff and again was instrumental in the development of something new—this time, a Radio Station on the Base. It was hugely successful! She also became an expert in Asian cooking. We children loved going up for school holidays. Geoff became very sick with Dengue Fever whilst in Butterworth which plagued him for the rest of his life.

In 1961, Geoffrey was posted to the Department of Defence in Canberra but in December 1963, he was posted to London for three years as Australian Joint Services Staff and Senior RAAF Representative London UK. Joy again relished the considerable entertaining she had to do.

My parents, Joy and Geoff, in the 1970s

Geoff's final posting was back in Canberra as Director General Service Personnel, Department of Air. In April 1968, he was discharged on a medical basis with the rank of Air Vice Marshal.

In the mid-1970s, my parents bought a camper van named 'Martha' and toured Canada, where Margaret was living at the time, and then the USA. Joy often expressed they were so lucky to have such a wonderful year together.

When they returned to Canberra Joy's interests increased, she became a tour guide at the National Library which she loved and also enjoyed regular bridge games and golf. She was a great fan of the University of the Third Age. Geoffrey's sudden death in May 1981 absolutely gutted her (it was way too soon—they had so much more to do together—she missed him every day). However, with steely determination, she carried on for another 16 odd years without him until she too sadly passed away on the 20 November 1997 with endometrial cancer.

No one can ever say that Joy sat still. She had a full, active life and many friends. She was and always will be a vital part of our lives.

Joy with her three children Marg, Ian and Tony

Chapter 16

Marjorie Nichols (Née Hankey)

Susan Read

Sue came to CCEGGS in high school. She established herself quickly as one of the clever people and one of my group of friends. We had a lot of fun partying and studying together as we moved from school to the ANU. During one summer holiday spent with the Nichols family at Merimbula, Sue's father taught me how to gut a fish and her mother showed me how to cook it. This proved very helpful in my later life. Mrs Nichols was also a driver and frequently transported us to parties and events. When doing so, she chatted about current affairs amongst other things. She was very learned and scholarly and we all admired her wisdom and intelligence.

Robbie Henderson

My mother, Marjorie, was born in Adelaide on 16 May 1920 to a family of South Australian pastoralists, on her father's side, and an English mother. Clara had come to Australia from Yorkshire after marrying Sydney Hankey, who she had met while he was studying the English wool trade after his service in the First World War. As the youngest son, Sydney did not gain any substantial wealth or landholdings from his family, and my mother soon moved to Melbourne with her parents.

In Melbourne, Marjorie attended Lauriston private girls' school, while her younger brother went to Melbourne Grammar. For much of their childhood, their father travelled in the western districts of Victoria, in his role as a wool valuer for The Australian Estates.

Marjorie did well in school, both in sports and academically and subsequently graduated with honours in Economics from Melbourne

University—highly unusual for a woman at the time. Given the accepted role and status of women pre-World War II, the support Marjorie's family provided for her tertiary education intrigues me, but my mother always portrayed it as something quite natural for her family to do.

Marjorie circa 1954

During the war, Marjorie answered the call for economics graduates to take the place of absent male public servants in Canberra. She worked as a Research Officer in the Bureau of Census and Statistics and, both from her stories and photos, it seems that she, at least, experienced quite an enjoyable war! Transport was by bicycle rather than car, and bike rides to places as far as the Cotter Dam appeared to have been a feature of summer outings.

Many of Marjorie's former male university colleagues and friends were serving overseas during the war years and a law student with whom she corresponded was David Nichols, by then a pilot in the RAAF. After David returned from the Middle East, they married in Melbourne in 1945—with my mother, a traditional bride, but in a borrowed wedding dress (Perhaps the reason she would never hear of me disposing of my wedding finery!).

Marjorie, of course, had to leave her Canberra job once she became engaged and her life in Melbourne was as a wife to David and a mother to me, daughter Susan, born in 1947. Meanwhile, David completed his law degree, with the help of government assistance provided to ex-servicemen, and then returned to the Air Force as a legal officer, which was to become his career.

A great tragedy in the life of both Marjorie and David was the death of their baby son, Andrew, in a car accident whilst David was on a work trip to Darwin. This was followed by a posting to RAAF Base Laverton, a 'change of scene' given by the Air Force to help the couple recover from their loss. I am not sure what my father made of his administrative duties there, but my mother certainly received support from the other officers' wives who welcomed her into Base life.

The small Nichols family moved from Victoria to Canberra in 1959, as part of the migration of Defence Force personnel to the new headquarters at Russell Hill. Initially, they lived in a government house in Campbell and Susan was enrolled in senior school at Canberra Church of England Girls' Grammar. However, David and Marjorie soon purchased a home of their own in Yarralumla, after the results of David's toil on the bare Campbell block kept being washed away by Canberra's spring rains.

Marjorie as a young woman

Once settled in their new home, with David increasingly involved in his legal work for the RAAF, Marjorie took up full time work again, back at the Bureau of Census and Statistics. (As my father was of the generation of men who felt their role was to be the breadwinner, I believe this move may have been recommended by our GP to 'keep my mother busy'.) If the aim was to lessen Marjorie's chronic anxiety, it appeared to work, as she was soon pregnant with another daughter. Amanda was born in 1961 to great joy.

Apart from her short time back in the workforce, Marjorie appeared to be satisfied with her life as a mother and Air Force officer's wife. She enjoyed entertaining and relished the social life of Canberra, as well as mothering young Mandy. During the 1960s, David took on more work responsibilities and Marjorie often managed the family on her own while David travelled to Vietnam for legal duties during the war years.

In 1964, having finished school, Susan travelled to the United States, living for 12 months with a Michigan family, the Peabodys, on an American Field Service (AFS) scholarship. After Susan returned and went to university, David retained an interest in AFS and was subsequently elected, as Australian representative, to the board of the scholarship scheme. Both in this capacity and as Director of Legal Services for the RAAF, David made many trips to the United States and southeast Asia, and Marjorie enjoyed travelling with him whenever she could.

The connection made via AFS with Susan's American family proved a fond and long-lasting one, which resulted in numerous reciprocal visits over the years. Marjorie loved showing Australia to the Peabodys and also visiting them in Michigan.

David retired from the Air Force in his mid-50s and soon after, Mandy completed school and moved to Adelaide to study medicine. David continued to undertake legal work in Canberra and Melbourne on a part-time basis for several years, pursuing gardening and food interests, whilst Marjorie loved entertaining and travelling overseas. In Canberra, the couple had a busy social life, enjoying activities with friends at the Food and Wine Club, Commonwealth Club and Austrian Club.

Although Marjorie was unusually highly educated for her generation of women, she never gave any indication to her daughters that she missed working outside the home. However, to Marjorie and David it was axiomatic that Susan and Mandy would both go to university. And, indeed, Marjorie was always entirely supportive of both her daughters' careers, and their lives as full-time working mothers.

Having been brought up by a determinedly English mother, Marjorie was a committed Anglophile all her life and supported Mandy's move from Australia to work in a London hospital. Marjorie particularly enjoyed a year she and David spent in England, living in a cottage in Sussex in the grounds of a property owned by a cousin of Dr Eric De Salis.

Marjorie was not so happy about leaving Canberra to live permanently on the Sunshine Coast of Queensland in the mid-1980s; but she did want to be near her older daughter, and particularly her young granddaughter, Sophie, born to Susan and Terry in 1979.

David, an asthmatic, loved the warmer weather of Queensland, but tragically, he died suddenly at the age of 71 after being hospitalised with an asthma attack. Marjorie, a dependent wife in many ways, was devastated by David's death and did not fully recover her enjoyment of life, although she travelled to Europe and spent time in Victoria with a dear friend from Melbourne University days. Unfortunately for her, a move back to Canberra was no longer a realistic choice, especially with one daughter now a single mother in Brisbane and the other establishing a family and a career as a doctor back in Adelaide.

In the years living in Buderim without David, Marjorie did charity work, played mah-jong and brushed up her schoolgirl French at the University of the Third Age. Although never fully accepting her Queensland location, Marjorie confidently drove herself to Brisbane to assist with the care of her by then teenage granddaughter Sophie, when Susan travelled with her work as a political pollster. Also, Marjorie did love visiting Adelaide and Mandy's two daughters, Claire and Natalie, but she always missed her friends and life in Canberra.

Sadly, although Marjorie lived another 20 plus years after David's death, her last few years were lost to dementia. Once it became obvious she needed care, Marjorie was able to make the decision to move to Adelaide, to be near Mandy and to live in a city she had always considered a second home. After five years in residence at an aged care home, increasingly 'away with the pixies', Marjorie died in 2014 aged 93.

The Writers

Anne De Salis

Anne has been a non-executive director for over 24 years. She is currently the Chair of the Audit Committee of MJD Foundation and has extensive experience in financial services, superannuation and governance issues. Her recent directorships include ME Bank Pty Ltd, a private bank owned by the Industry Super Funds, and Indigenous Pastoral Enterprises Pty Ltd, a subsidiary of the Indigenous Land Corporation, which oversights the sustainability of and training outcomes for some 14 Northern Australian pastoral enterprises.

As a member of Chief Executive Women, an experienced coach with Executive Coaching International and a mentor with McCarthy Mentoring, she continues to support young women executives and aspiring board directors.

During her career, she held senior executive and leadership positions in the public and private sectors, gaining deep experience in government, policymaking, stakeholder management and corporate culture as well as developing successful business strategies and high performing teams. For more than 10 years, Anne worked with large Australian businesses, mostly in roles with 'bottom line' responsibilities. She established and led an on-line retail financial services business for AMP Limited in 2000 and as General Manager ran AMP's large corporate superannuation business for four years. She was also a direct report of AMP's CEO and General Counsel with responsibility for Government Affairs, and spent two years in MBF's senior executive team.

Before joining AMP, Anne enjoyed several years working as Senior Adviser to the then Prime Minister, the Right Hon Paul Keating, in Parliament House in Canberra. She joined the Keating Office from the Commonwealth Treasury, where she worked as an economic adviser to the Federal Government. In 1991, she became the first woman to join Treasury's senior executive service since Federation.

Anne has held a variety of board appointments, including Funds SA, SAS Trustee Corporation, the NSW TAFE Commission, Centre for Policy Development, NSW Financial Institutions Commission, AMP Super Limited, Veterinary Science Foundation and the University of Canberra Council.

She has also acted as a trustee of CEDA and been a member of the Walkley Awards Media Council. In 1993–4, she was a member of the Council of the Order of Australia, which selects recipients for the highest awards made to Australian citizens.

In 2002, Anne became a Fellow of the Australian Institute of Company Directors and the following year, was awarded a Centenary of Federation medal for her contribution to business. She has a BA (Economics) and MA from the Australian National University, CM, FAICD. She lives in Sydney and has two children, Nina and David and two grandchildren.

Diana Cooper

Di was born in Melbourne in 1946 and lived there until her parents left for UK when she was four. They lived in London, where her brother was born, and subsequently Bonn for a total of five years. The family returned to Canberra when she was nine and she went to the Canberra Church of England Girls Grammar School. At 11, her parents were sent to Singapore and she went to boarding school in Mittagong for almost four years, which were hard due to the isolation of the school. When the family returned, she finished the last two years of school back in Canberra at the same Grammar School, where she was reunited with old friends with whom she has remained close ever since.

She went to Vienna with the family after finishing school but returned to work in Canberra when 19 years old. While in Austria, she discovered skiing, which became her lifelong sporting interest. After a stint in Sydney working in the fashion industry, she returned to Canberra, where she made a short-lived marriage at 26. The aftermath was challenging, but also a happy new beginning.

Di undertook secretarial work at the ANU while studying for a B.A. in Social Sciences. She then worked in three universities where she undertook careers counselling which she loved. She undertook further part time study at ANU, completing a Litt.B. in the Sociology of Australia's mental health laws. She subsequently gained employment at the newly formed National Training Board working to bring about Australia's new national industry training system, which once again, she enjoyed immensely. When the NTB closed, she worked on contract for a few years. However unable to regain full time employment, she retired at 58.

A very happy and active time followed, in particular at the University of the Third Age, but also with short trips overseas. When her parents passed away, she was able to buy a small flat in Sydney where she had always wanted to live. One of the major benefits has been living close to friends in Canberra and also those who now live in Sydney or who visit from elsewhere.

Bill Fisher

Bill Fisher is a Canberra native, born in the now exploded-and-imploded Canberra Community Hospital in Acton, now the site of the Museum of Australia. The family's home was in Deakin, he went to Canberra Grammar, did an Honours degree in Economics at ANU and joined the then Department of External Affairs (now known as DFAT) in the diplomatic intake of 1968. He and his wife, Kerry, met during their time together at ANU's Bruce Hall (now also demolished); they recently celebrated their 50th wedding anniversary.

On leaving ANU, Bill Fisher was appointed as a senior officer in the Department of Foreign Affairs and Trade. He served most recently as the Australian Ambassador for Counter-Terrorism (2013–14), the Prime Minister's Special Envoy to the Francophone States (2011–2013), High Commissioner to Canada (2005–2008), Ambassador to France (2000–2005) and Algeria, Morocco and Mauritania, Ambassador to Thailand (1997–2000), Ambassador to Israel (1990–94) and previously as Charge d'Affaires to Iran, Consul General Honolulu and Micronesia, Consul General to the New Hebrides, Consul General in New Caledonia, with earlier postings also in the Australian Embassy in Laos and in the Australian Missions to the United Nations in Geneva and in New York.

In Canberra, Bill held a number of senior positions in the Department of Foreign Affairs, including as Head of the Africa and Middle East Division, the Consular and Security Division, the International Organisations and Legal Division and Head of the Defence Branch of the Department of the Prime Minister and Cabinet.

He is currently a Visiting Fellow, College of Diplomacy at the ANU College of Asia and the Pacific where he is doing policy work on the Pacific, with visits back to Francophone Africa for the government and various other interesting organisations. Between lectures delivered at ANU and DFAT, he makes radio and TV appearances for the ABC, SBS and Voice of America.

Bill is married to Kerry, and they have one daughter.

Kerry Fisher

Kerry Fisher is Jean Gulson's eldest daughter. Born in Goulburn and educated at PLC Goulburn, she was the first of her family to go to University, and to do science. Her uni days were spent at Bruce Hall, the first of the ANU residential colleges, now demolished—thanks ANU's keen sense of history. At Bruce Hall, she met her husband, Bill Fisher, with whom she celebrated this year their 50th wedding anniversary.

Having specialised in biological sciences during her degree Kerry went on to do a Diploma of Education at Sydney University. This led on, after a brief spell teaching high school science, to a job as Research Assistant at the John Curtin School of Medical Research at ANU. This career was curtailed when husband Bill joined the Diplomatic Service and the newly married couple were sent to their first posting at the Australian Mission to the United Nations in Geneva. Living in Geneva required French, so Kerry did a Diploma in French language and Literature at Geneva University. Her proficiency in French turned out to be a useful skill because several of her and Bill's future postings were in French speaking countries. That included their next one, Laos in its wartime pre-communist period when French was still the official language. She also took the opportunity while there to learn Lao, an effort which came in handy years later when she went on a posting to Bangkok were she learnt Thai.

Returning to Canberra, Kerry decided on a change in direction from science to something more relevant to her life in diplomatic postings—she undertook a Bachelor of Asian Studies at ANU. Kerry again took the opportunity to start learning Persian and, more generally Arabic writing. She and Bill were then posted twice to the South Pacific—Noumea and Port Vila—again, French-speaking. As the spouse of the Head of Post, Kerry had her work cut out in filling that role with the local communities. She was especially interested in development issues, and so when the next return to Canberra came around, she got another research assistant job at ANU, this time with the Development Studies Centre. Other postings followed including Bangkok, Paris and Ottawa where she developed a passion for cross-country skiing.

A difficult posting followed; Tehran during the revolution and the Iran-Iraq war. Tehran was followed by Honolulu, where Kerry and Bill's daughter, Adelaide, was born. A delightful period of parenthood in a delightful place for five years made up for the tensions of Tehran. But that ended as Bill was sent as Ambassador to Israel at the time of the first Gulf War, leading to some dramatic moments of evacuation and separation.

On final return to Australia, Kerry and Bill were based in Melbourne for a few years where daughter Adelaide was at Melbourne University and so the family was together once more. Melbourne for Kerry was sorely impacted by a struggle with breast cancer, ultimately successful but hugely unpleasant at the time. Kerry and Bill finally returned to Canberra in 2013 after an absence of 15 years. It is truly home.

Margaret Furnell

Margaret Furnell was born on the 6 April 1946 in Perth WA to Joy and Geoff Hartnell. Geoff was commanding officer at the Pearce Air Force Base at the time. It seems that her life from day one was destined to involve change. The result has been interesting and never dull!

Marg's childhood was spent at many Air Force bases throughout Australia and overseas. This also meant numerous schools—always the new girl! Her brothers were sent to boarding school for stability, but as a female, the perception at that time was to prepare her for life as a wife and mother.

After she completed school at the Canberra Church of England Girls Grammar School, Marg was obliged to accompany her parents to London where her father was based at Australia House in Defence. Her innate travel bug and love of languages took Marg to Paris where she attended the Sorbonne and lived as an au pair with a French family. She absolutely loved it! After that, she did an exchange with an Italian family in Turin.

Sadly for Marg, she was enjoying Europe far too much and was forced to return to Australia with her parents. However, the love of travel did not diminish so she applied to Qantas Airways as a flight hostess. The next couple of years Marg spent exploring the world and being paid for it. For her, an idyllic lifestyle.

Marg married a Canadian in the early 1970s and had two children. They moved to Canada to live in Edmonton, Alberta—far too cold! They compromised and moved to Southern California. Marg's children spent their school and university years in Southern Cal. Marg rekindled her ties to Australia by re-joining Qantas as the customer service manager at LAX. She did not realise how homesick she was and returned to Sydney to live in the early 1990s.

Marg retired from Qantas in the late '90s and was asked to assist in setting up a new subsidiary of Qantas called Australian Airlines. The airline was based in Cairns far north QLD. A wonderful little airline but sadly, it only functioned for approximately five years before Jetstar took over!

Life in far north QLD was very enticing and Marg decided to stay on and live a dream she had always had of owning an interior design and homewares store. During one of her travels down south on a buying trip, she re-met an old flame from school days and approximately four years ago, they decided to get married. Geoff moved from the south coast of New South Wales to the hot tropics!

Marg says it is almost time to retire again from her business and enjoy more travel—throughout Australia, New Zealand, Asia, Europe and also to see more of her beautiful grandchildren in Toronto, Canada and Geoff's eight grandchildren in Canberra and the Gold Coast.

Pam Gray

Pam Gray is a clinical psychologist in private practice (now largely retired) living in Bargara, Queensland with her husband Brian (an academic researcher in education and psychology). In retirement, Brian has been restoring a yacht and Pam works with a few clients and, for around a month a year, at 6-star spa retreats in Thailand as a visiting consultant where she offers guests 'Counselling, Hypnosis and Art therapy'.

In her earlier adult life, Pam lived and worked (initially as a teacher, then as a psychologist) mostly in Canberra in the Australian Capital Territory (where she went to school and university) and in Alice Springs and Darwin in the Northern Territory. Before she went into private practice for many years, she ran the Counselling Service at the University of Canberra.

She has two sons and a young grandson.

Life is good.

Robyn (Robbie) Henderson

On completion of her initial studies at the ANU, Robbie left Canberra to work as a biochemist in Sydney. Her time in Sydney was brief and in the early '70s, she returned to Canberra with her then partner Steve Walmsley, had two children, Claudia and Joshua, and studied political science and women's studies. She worked briefly as a teacher in the United Kingdom.

An activist career followed as the women's movement flourished culminating in her election as a member of the ACT Legislative Assembly. On returning to Sydney in 1985, Robbie spent the following thirty years working in the non-government sector and the NSW, ACT and Commonwealth governments. She was the National Director of the Institute of Public Administration Australia, Chief of Staff to the NSW Minister for Women and Fair Trading, Faye Lo Po and Director General of the NSW Department for Women.

In 2004, she joined RAMSI as an advisor to the Solomon Islands' Prime Minister and Head of the Cabinet Office, and in 2008 worked as an advisor to the national police (PNTL) in Dili, Timor-Leste.

Robbie holds a BSc, BA, MLitt in Cultural Studies, LLB and an Associate Diploma in Labour Studies.

She now lives in Canberra with her husband Geoff Evans, a farmer and works in the public sector. Robbie has four grandchildren, from whom she has learnt a lot. She spends as much time as possible with them and her extended family.

Meredith Hinchliffe

Meredith Hinchliffe has been involved with the arts since 1977 when she began work with the Crafts Council of the ACT. She is now a freelance curator and writer and an arts advocate.

Meredith was a contributor to The Canberra Times from 1978 to 2009 and writes review articles of crafts and visual arts exhibitions and books. She also writes about issues of importance to the arts. She has written articles for a number of journals, including the National Library News, Smarts, Pottery in Australia—now Journal of Australian Ceramics, Craft Arts International, Fibre Forum, and Ceramic Art and Perception. She now reviews craft exhibitions for City News.

She was the full time Executive Director of the National Campaign for the Arts Australia Ltd from July 1996 until August 1997, when the organisation was wound up due to lack of funding. From August 1997 to December 1999, she worked as a freelance consultant.

She was appointed Executive Officer of Museums Australia, the national professional association for museum workers and museums in July 2002. From July 2008 to April 2009, she was the inaugural Executive Officer of the Donald Horne Institute for Cultural Heritage at the University of Canberra.

Meredith worked as Public Arts Project Officer for arts ACT for a year and has managed several public art installation projects. In 2013, Meredith curated an exhibition of Fred Ward furniture at the then Gallery of Australian Design. She has curated several other exhibitions of textiles, furniture and ceramics. Meredith has served on the boards of a number of local arts organisations in the visual and performing arts.

In 2000, she was awarded an ACT Women's Award in recognition of her significant contribution to the ACT community in the arts. In 2011, she was awarded an Australia Day medal by the National Gallery of Australia. She was an active member of the Women's Electoral Lobby from 1972, and she maintains an active interest in feminist issues.

Helen McBride

After completing her schooling in Canberra, Helen moved to Adelaide where she attended Wattle Park Teachers' College and taught lower primary children. In 1968, she married Phillip (Flip) McBride, a local farmer and commenced a new life as a grazier on a property 60 km north of Kingston in SE SA. After her son, Nicholas, and daughter, Kate, were born, Helen undertook relief teaching, but found the things she enjoyed about teaching were missing in relief work.

In 1978, Helen moved to a family property, Conmurra, 40 km east of Kingston. Her second daughter, Georgie, arrived later that year. She subsequently enjoyed 22 years at Conmurra where she kept the books for the grazing business and was busy with the daily running of the family and the property. She undertook several TAFE courses and voluntary work in the district.

Helen participated on local committees, Mothers and Babies, kindergarten, and school canteen and was the local and regional president of Red Cross, local, the region president of the golf club and on the local and regional TAFE council for a number of years. She has enjoyed playing competitive tennis for over 40 years and social bridge. Helen and Flip moved into retirement to Kingston, SA in 2000. She has four grandchildren, Jack, Annabel, Philip and Seb. Helen's son Nick is the Member for MacKillop in the SA Parliament and runs the family's grazing property.

Louise Moran

Louise Moran is sometimes told she's very like her mother, a compliment she treasures but feels she falls short of most of the time. She is the eldest of three, Michael and Hugh being three and six years younger respectively, and was born in Oxford in 1947. Louise was nearly five when the family moved to Canberra, went to primary school there and on to a ghastly boarding school in Sydney from which she emerged, somewhat battered, to start university—and life—in 1964. That first degree (BA in history and politics) at the ANU was later followed by postgraduate qualifications in educational administration and a PhD in higher education history from the University of British Columbia.

After a couple of years of travel, Louise settled into a career in university administration and then, from 1979, distance education, particularly at the then-new Deakin University in Victoria where she ran the distance education program and academic planning for it through Deakin's first decade. From the mid-1980s, she added international education to her portfolio, as Australia opened up its doors to fee-paying overseas students. Both fields gave her numerous opportunities for international travel and she started working on international projects as well as national ones.

She moved to South Australia in 1995 but in 1997 decided enough was enough; universities had changed in ways she could no longer bear. Instead, after a stint in northern Sweden, she moved home to Canberra (one of the best decisions of her life), set up a consulting company and spent the next decade advising universities, Australian governments, vocational education systems and international agencies on flexible learning and international education. Enough really was enough in 2006 and she 'retired' to focus more on volunteering, travel for fun (versus work), gardening, cooking and, increasingly, caring for Jean. She treasures that last decade of Jean's life as a particularly special period. She reckons that if she can age even half as well as Jean did, she'll do well.

Susan Read

Like other sons and daughters in this book, Susan spent her teenage and early adult years in Canberra. From 1966 to 1968, she studied for an Arts Degree at the Australian National University, majoring in Political Science and Psychology. An M.A. in Political Sociology followed later.

Susan's subsequent career built on her ANU studies, covering academic teaching (in Canberra, Sydney and Brisbane); advertising research (with J. Walter Thompson, Sydney); commercial market research (in Sydney and Brisbane); and finally, government service in Queensland's Department of the Premier and Cabinet.

Throughout Susan's time with three market research companies—ANOP, AGB McNair and UMR Research—a consistent and major client was the Australian Labor Party, both federally and at state level. Research into Australians' political attitudes and the testing of advertisements for election campaigns formed the central focus of most of her working life.

Like many mothers, Susan had a period of part-time work after a move from Sydney to Queensland's Sunshine Coast with her husband and small daughter in 1982. But the end of her marriage six years later necessitated a move to Brisbane and the continuance of full-time market research. The taxing demands of frequent elections and travel throughout Australia saw Susan opt for the Queensland Public Service in 1999. She retired from the Department of the Premier and Cabinet in 2011 and now enjoys the life of a retirement community, her grandchildren, volunteering and leisure travel.

Vee Saunders

Vee Saunders is a child of empire, while the British Empire still existed. Her earliest memories are of Singapore, an island which influenced greatly her attitudes and opinions. At eight years old, she was sent to the cold eastern coast of Scotland to boarding school for nine years. She received an almost classic education there, leaving after completing four GCE 'A' levels, the British equivalent of the Australian tertiary entrance. She came to Australia in 1965 and attended the Australian National University studying English Literature, History and French. After her incarceration at boarding school, the temptation of university social life proved more exciting than her studies forcing her to abandon her studies and join the Commonwealth Public Service in the Department of Territories.

In 1968, Vee married Denis Saunders and moved from Canberra to Perth. She continued to work with a government department there till her first pregnancy. With a husband engaged in biological fieldwork on a regular basis, she decided to be the constant in her two daughters' lives and became a stay-at-home mother. She supported her husband's career, often entertaining visiting scientists, Australian and overseas. She pursued various careers once her daughters were at school—she set up a small catering business, worked in a wine cellar of a local vineyard and for a short time, acted as a kindergarten assistant. Vee was active in school affairs, serving on the parents' body for the school, taking part in working bees and often helping out in the library.

Vee enrolled at Murdoch University to study linguistic and cultural studies but was unable to fully complete the degree when her confidence levels plunged despite very good results. Throughout her life, Vee has had an interest in writing, in cooking and in current affairs. With her husband, she is involved in philanthropic issues.

Denis Saunders

Denis Saunders BSc Hons (ANU) PhD (UWA) is an animal ecologist and conservation biologist. He is a former CSIRO Chief Research Scientist, past President of WWF-Australia, and currently Chair of the Sara Halvedene Foundation, a member of the Wentworth Group of Concerned Scientists, and an honorary fellow with CSIRO Land and Water in Canberra. He has studied the ecology, behaviour and taxonomy of cockatoos, the ecology of island bird communities, and the conservation of bird communities in agricultural landscapes. From 1968 to the present, he has conducted an ecological and behavioural study of the endangered Carnaby's Cockatoo, an endemic of Southwestern Australia.

In 1998, he was awarded the International Society for Conservation Biology's Individual in Government award for making 'significant, meaningful and lasting contributions to conservation biology'. In 1999, he received the International Association for Landscape Ecology's Distinguished Scholarship Award for 'exceptional contributions to the development of landscape ecology as a science and a practice'. In 2000, he was Highly Commended in the Australian Prime Minister's Environment Award for 'Outstanding Individual Achievement for highly significant contribution to the research and practice of biodiversity conservation'.

He was made a Member of the General Division of the Order of Australia in 2005 for 'service to nature conservation, particularly through the study of Australian birds and the development of landscape ecology in Australia'. In 2006, he was awarded the D. L. Serventy Medal by Birds Australia for 'outstanding contributions to publication in the science of ornithology in the Australasian region'. In 2014, he was awarded the Royal Zoological Society of New South Wales' Certificate of Commendation for service to conservation. He is married to Vee and has two daughters, Samantha and Romayne, and two grandsons, Archie and Will.

Stephen Walmsley

Stephen Walmsley a graduate of the ANU law school, has practised law for over 30 years, initially as a solicitor, later as a barrister, and was appointed Senior Counsel in NSW in 1997. From 2001 to 2013, he was a judge of the District Court of NSW.

He is co-author of Professional Liability in Australia (Walmsley, Abadee, Zipser and Sirtes, Thomson LBC, 2016, 3rd ed), and author of The Trials of Justice Murphy (LexisNexis, 2017).

He is married to Leonie Flannery. He was formerly married to Robbie Henderson, with whom he had two children, Claudia and Joshua.

Donelle Wheeler

Donelle left Canberra to go to the University of Sydney. After teaching for a very short time, she travelled, married and had Victoria, working all the while, eventually becoming a bureaucrat, in NSW and the Commonwealth. She worked for three ALP Ministers as an adviser and senior adviser and then joined AusAID and retired from there.

In retirement from the full-time workforce, she's been President of the Australian National Committee for UN Women and continues to work occasionally on international development projects or gender equality. She failed to inherit her mother's domestic arts skills.

Philip Wheeler

After leaving school in 1963, Philip managed to eke out an enjoyable career as a full-time university student for 16 years at the ANU and Oxford University, picking up smatterings of law, economics and classics along the way.

As an adult (eventually), he joined the NSW Public Service and attempted, somewhat futilely, to uphold the tradition of fearless, independent and impartial advice to government in the face of increasing politicisation of the bureaucracy. He served as NSW State Secretary and National Secretary of the Institute of Public Administration Australia (formerly RAIPA, then RIPAA and finally IPAA), being awarded a Fellowship of the Institute, as well as a Public Service Medal.

In 2006, he embarked on overseas development assistance work in the South Pacific, first in the Solomon Islands, and subsequently for more than a decade in

PNG, working on programs to strengthen public sector governance in central agencies and in the judiciary.

Philip was married to Donelle and is the proud father of Victoria who has followed both her parents (and her Wheeler grandfather) into public service.

CPSIA information can be obtained
at www.ICGtesting.com
Printed in the USA
LVHW081726261021
701610LV00007B/92

9 781528 999434